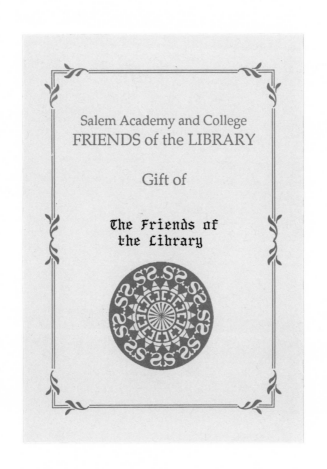

Toward Wholeness

in Paule Marshall's Fiction

Toward Wholeness in Paule Marshall's Fiction

JOYCE PETTIS

UNIVERSITY PRESS OF VIRGINIA   *Charlottesville and London*

THE UNIVERSITY PRESS OF VIRGINIA
Copyright © 1995 by the Rector and Visitors
of the University of Virginia

First published 1995

Library of Congress Cataloging-in-Publication Data

Pettis, Joyce Owens.
Toward wholeness in Paule Marshall's fiction / Joyce Pettis.
p.   cm.
Includes bibliographical references and index.
ISBN 0-8139-1614-3 (cloth)
1. Marshall, Paule, 1929–   —Knowledge—Psychology.
2. Women and literature—United States—History—20th
century.   3. Whole and parts (Psychology) in literature.
4. Afro-Americans in literature.   5. Caribbean Area—In
literature.   6. Afro-Americans—Psychology.   7. Psychology in
literature.   I. Title.
PS3563.A7223Z83   1995
813'.54—dc20   94–48916
                                                                        CIP

Printed in the United States of America

For my ancestors,

who taught me more than they realize

Lillian Hill Gibbs, Mamie Collins Owens,

and Odessa Alexander Wrighton

and

For my mother, Victoria Elizabeth Owens,

whose teachings will never die

Contents

Acknowledgments

Because most academic works germinate in the intellectual setting of the workplace, I will appropriately begin by expressing my appreciation for colleagues there who have encouraged and enabled this work. John Bassett, the chair of the English department at North Carolina State University when I began this project, thoughtfully assisted its progress in many ways, including his part in the summer stipend I received from the College of Humanities and Social Science Humanities Foundation. Using the initiative of the provost's office to assist African-American faculty research, Lawrence Clark and Augustus Witherspoon provided funds for a research assistant. Julie Moody worked diligently and creatively in that capacity.

I also have benefited from the camaraderie of three groups of scholars—the "Wintergreen Collective," my mountain retreat friends, and annual attendees at meetings of the African-American Popular Culture Area of the Popular Culture Association and of the College Language Association. Among these groups, I am grateful for the special assistance of Ronald Dorris, Ronald Foreman, Joanne Gabbin, Sandra Y. Govan, J. Lee Greene, Trudier Harris, Helen Houston, Dolan Hubbard, Carole Marsh-Lockett, Patsy Perry, Phil Royster, Harry Shaw, and Loretta Gilchrist Woodard. Over the years, they have assisted my study of Marshall by inviting essays or presentations about her, recommending me for fellowships, including me on academic panels, or offering encouragement and enthusiasm. Jerry Barrax, Gay Wilentz, and Karla Holloway read excerpted chapters, provided the wonderful models of their own work, and offered advice and motivation. I am profoundly grateful for their encouragement.

The Friday Night Women, an avid group of readers, have been invaluable to my well-being during this project. They have cheered my small successes and made some difficult periods endurable. Among them, Sandra Campbell reminded me that I needed to work at my own speed and listened to my comparative essay on Avey Johnson and Macon Dead, Jr., when she might have been sightseeing in England. Gracie Miller and Anita Miles, devotees of good fiction, especially of Marshall, have been constant supporters.

Writing and research are time consuming. When their pursuit takes priority, family members may have to reschedule activities. My son, Daryl, has always given me the time and silence that I required, as did my husband, Bobby, before his death. My gratitude to Myrtle, Bertron Don, Carla June, Donna, and Victoria, who have lovingly given me many second chances when I needed them. Corianne Denise, masquerading as a three-year-old angel, made me reset priorities.

Enoch Charles Temple, with whom I have a second marriage, has filled the silences and been totally supportive during the completion of this book.

Finally, I am immensely grateful to Paule Marshall for her gracious and cooperative assistance and for giving readers the wonderful gift of her fiction.

Toward Wholeness

in Paule Marshall's Fiction

Introduction

Progression, momentum, and culmination form the concept of a journey and are useful in thinking about Paule Marshall's fiction. Journeys are significant for many characters in *Brown Girl, Brownstones; Soul Clap Hands and Sing; The Chosen Place, the Timeless People; Praisesong for the Widow;* and *Daughters.* The most significant travel establishes cultural connections among people of the African diaspora and advances the traveler from spiritual moribundity to spiritual reclamation. Through multidimensional characters and situations in the United States and the Caribbean, each work reproduces patterns of race, gender, and class along with other forces that fracture the psyche. Marshall uses the journey motif to communicate the necessity of movement away from the debilitation caused by fracturing. Her characters travel, literally and metaphorically, but only one of them reaches the desired destination at the novel's end. In *Praisesong,* Avatara Johnson, an elderly widow, finally reaches the goal toward which Marshall's fiction has journeyed for twenty-four years. It is a small island named Carriacou, where remnants of West Africa are remembered and form an active part of the islanders' customs. It is where spiritual reintegration occurs. This book will examine Marshall's canon as her provocative passage to culmination, where psychic transformation becomes possible.

Daughters confirms that the spiritual journey of Avatara Johnson in *Praisesong* brings closure to a particular vision that has animated Marshall's work. Although fragmented characters exist in this novel, its focus shifts away from their spiritual recovery. Its psychically centered characters are not limited to those spiritually whole ancestors who appear in earlier novels. *Daughters* is nonetheless a significant part of this work because it continues to explore the consequences of colonialism in the Caribbean, the intersections of race, gender, and class, and the behavior of psychically whole characters as positive agents of community.

The fractured psyche, defined and discussed in chapter 1, identifies a motif that, like the journey, has constituted a primary concept in Marshall's work. The presence of the fractured psyche has increased the richness and multidimensionality of the experiences she chronicles and has helped to anchor her work historically. Her inclusive fiction incorporates subjects such as men and women in urban and rural labor forces, the individual and the community, immigrants and assimilation in adopted countries, and conflicts between illusion and reality. Her work offers insight into personal relations, including those between husbands and wives, same-sex friends, mothers and daughters, and fathers and daughters.[1] These relationships are complicated by fracturing, particularly in the areas of individual and cultural identity, individual and cultural alienation, and spiritual moribundity.

The journey motif complements and enhances the geographic sweep of Marshall's fiction and becomes crucial in the reciprocity between her texts and the cultures represented in them.[2] The West Indians in *Brown Girl* are immigrants from Barbados; an American research team in *The Chosen Place* relocates to the fictional island of Bourne; the Afro-Caribbean protagonist Merle Kinbona immigrates to London for her college education and many years later plans to travel to East Africa; the Connecticut-born Estelle establishes her life on the Caribbean island of Triunion and sends her Triunion-born daughter to Connecticut during her adolescence; Avatara's vacation cruise from New York places her in Grenada and Carriacou. The novellas of *Soul Clap Hands and Sing* are set in North America, South America, and the Caribbean. This geographic sweep is central to Marshall's fiction in emphasizing the widespread nature of fracturing that originated with a displaced West African population during the slave trade.[3]

The Chosen Place expands in scope to include an exploration of the fates of the white descendants of traders. Are these people, whose economic and class position was secured through the purchase and sale of Africans and related import and export industries, ignorant about or unscarred by that history? How might they redeem themselves, although they had no direct role in the accretion of their wealth and inherited power? Through Harriet Amron, a WASP from New England whose inheritance originated with profits from the trade, Marshall depicts an angle that is often underrepresented. As a member of the research team traveling to Bourne Island, Harriet personally journeys back, but she arrives at an impasse between the personal and historical.

Marshall stated that in designing *The Chosen Place*, she wanted "to have a kind of vehicle that looked at the relationship of the West to the rest of us. So I hoped that the novel would not solely be seen as a novel about the West Indies, even though it's set there, but a novel that reflects what is happening to all of us in the Diaspora in our encounter with these metropolitan powers, the power of Europe and the power of America."[4] Using character, ritual, and symbols of technology, Bourne Island becomes one of many places in Marshall's canon where she dissects intricate relationships that produce fracturing. The diversity of this topographic representation underscores Marshall's commitment to education about the African diaspora and her acknowledgment of a worldwide black community of African descendants.[5] Although she does not situate characters in West Africa, its presence hovers as the origin of cultural identity.

This book is structured to follow Marshall's movement toward spiritual wholeness. Fragmentation is located in the historical experiences of black people of the African diaspora, and the fractured psyche is defined as the rending and mutilation of human spirit, a process that represents an unavoidable consequence of traumatic cultural displacement. The continuing presence of the fractured psyche indicates progressive alienation in a culture hostile to African Americans and Afro-Caribbeans. This perpetual conflict originates in the difference between European cosmological systems and African systems. The social reality for descendants of West Africans in the United States and the Caribbean, defined by European cosmology, privileges qualities that are alien to an African cultural orientation.

Evidence of fracturing and alienation that can be linked to opposition between Eurocentric culture and African-derived culture is supported by the research of numerous psychologists who work from an Afrocentric perspective. The work of Na'im Akbar and Joseph A. Baldwin underpins cultural analysis of Marshall's fractured men and women in conflict with their social reality. Akbar's and Baldwin's research, discussed in chapter 1, also verifies the consequences of these problems. This volume also cites the work of Gerald Gregory Jackson, who links evidence of fracturing with cultural differences between Africans and Europeans. Robert Blauner's study of differences between immigrants and colonized people lends credibility to the discussion of the sociocultural results of displacement and bondage.

Several words describe the ideal postfractured state—*spiritual wholeness, regeneration, reintegration,* and *reclamation.* All of these terms speak to the restoration of wholeness, which means that the spirit is gathered up, healed, and revealed unto itself (see chapters 1 and 4). Marshall's trilogy—*Brown Girl, The Chosen Place,* and *Praisesong*—is discrete not only in its trajectory toward this ideal but also in its location of the healing within the black cultural and communal matrix. The emphasis on Marshall's progressive thematic vision is substantiated by the female protagonists in her trilogy. The journey is instrumental to all of them, but in the first two books the protagonists only stand poised for their most significant travel at the conclusion of the text. Not until Avatara Johnson's extensive literal and metaphorical travels in *Praisesong* does Marshall culminate journeying with embracing one's cultural origins and healing a fractured psyche. Spiritual wholeness is finally attained.

Spiritual wholeness, reintegration, reclamation, and *spirituality* are used interchangeably in this discussion to designate the desirable end of a splintered psyche. The term *spirituality* is employed in its West African cultural sense as an embodiment of dynamic energy separate from the physical body but essential to its well-being, both physically and emotionally. Spirituality is acknowledged by psychologists and others who study traditional African culture. In chapter 1, the research of Linda James Myers and Dominique Zahan confirms intellectually that spirituality is a dynamic entity in the experience of descendants of Africans. Margaret Washington Creel links spirituality with the African worldview, writing that it "affected one's whole system of being, embracing the consciousness, social interactions, and attitudes, fears and dispositions of the community at large" (72). The significance of the term *spiritual wholeness* within this context justifies its appropriation as the desired goal in the journeys undertaken in Marshall's fiction.

Several theoretical perspectives shape my reading of the novels discussed here. I am primarily indebted to black feminist practice and feminist literary theory. The historical and cultural resources that invigorate my readings of Marshall's fiction—my contextual focus, in other words—reflects Deborah McDowell's idea that a study of black women's literature should "expose the conditions under which literature is produced, published, and reviewed." This procedure is "not only useful but necessary to Black feminist critics" ("New Directions," 192). Establishing the cultural context and identifying the forces that shape the existence of black men and women is an essential step in their representation in criticism. Paula Giddings's *When and Where I Enter*, Patricia Hill Collins's *Black Feminist Thought*, Jacqueline Jones's *Labor of Love, Labor of Sorrow*, Deborah K. King's "Multiple Jeopardy, Multiple Consciousness," and Bonnie Thornton Dill's essays all prove vital in sustaining a black feminist perspective and in incorporating historical and sociological findings to inform literary analysis. Just as important, these studies were instrumental in furthering the identification of race, gender, and class inequities. Because significant parts of this book emphasize black workers as exploited and therefore fractured, Marxist feminist criticism also offers viable ways of interpreting the relationship between labor and exploitation and of drawing conclusions about the state of the psyche in that connection. Josephine Donovan's *Feminist Theory: The Intellectual Traditions of American Feminism* provides useful insights into Marxist feminist ideology.

Marshall's status in American literature constitutes an underlying motivation for this book. Scholars of African-American and Afro-Caribbean literature, avid readers of these works, and many contemporary American novelists consider her among the premier American writers. Her work is taught internationally. Nevertheless, significant numbers of Americans knowledgeable about literature remain ignorant of Marshall. Consequently, this volume seeks to increase her much-deserved visibility to a multicultural audience. In the afterword to *Brown Girl, Brownstones,* Mary Helen Washington wrote that "just now—in the 1980s—[Marshall is] being discovered," although by that time she had authored three major books (323). Since 1981, Marshall has published two more substantial novels, and black women's fiction has received increased critical attention, some of which has been directed at Marshall's sustained and serious work. Based on her inclusion in theses and dissertations and in chapters in book-length critical studies, particularly those whose terrain includes the diaspora, interest in her work is accelerating. *Daughters* has perhaps introduced her to another audience, both through television appearances—where Marshall talked about her work—and through its publication during a period of lively interest in fiction by black women. Most significantly, receiving the prestigious MacArthur Award in 1992 has certainly enhanced her status in American letters.

Marshall's membership in both the Afro-Caribbean and African-American communities appreciably widens her audience. Carol Davies, Daryl Dance, and Edward Brathwaite, all cited in chapter 1, are among those who claim her cross-culturally. Brathwaite, in fact, cites *The Chosen Place* as "a significant contribution to the literature of the West Indies" and praises its scope and value ("Rehabilitations," 126).

One means of evaluating Marshall's status in the tradition of African-American letters is to view her fiction in relation to her fellow writers. Therefore, this book will juxtapose Marshall's work with the fiction of other women writers and discuss its articulation within a women's literary tradition. The authors with whom she is compared include Pauline Hopkins, Frances Ellen Watkins Harper, Nella Larsen, Jessie Fauset, Zora Neale Hurston (representing an early tradition in black women's fiction) and Ann Petry, Gwendolyn Brooks, Kristin Hunter, Sarah

Wright, and Toni Morrison (evoking later style). Although several themes, images, and situations in the fiction of these writers mesh with Marshall's work, her distinction among them is established through the unity of her measured tread toward psychic reintegration and through her inclusion of the African diaspora. This comparative assessment is essential to a claim for enhancing Marshall's status in American and African-American letters.

Although Marshall's vision of spiritual wholeness serves as the unifying entity of her work, her fiction is neither parochial nor myopic. Thus, this book deliberately avoids analyzing her fiction chronologically and follows instead a topical approach.

Chapter 1 establishes the perspective for an investigation of the fractured psyche in Marshall's fiction, notes the phenomenon's presence in the work of other writers, and points out Marshall's distinctiveness in her development of it. Relevant biographical and literary connections are established because they underscore pertinent diasporic connections in the novels. Her position among women writers in African-American literary tradition is also discussed.

Chapter 2 has its basis in the initial disruption of African communities. Community as a vital entity in the experiences of black people is equally important in Marshall's fiction. Where people group themselves, how they identify with the land in Third World settings, and how they manage their survival in merciless urban cities is connected with the well-being of the psyche. Marshall's characters identify certain spaces as psychological havens; that is, the seclusion and psychocultural safety of the setting outweighs its physicality. The chapter also examines configurations of ritual, legacy, history, and survival in the community in *The Chosen Place* and explores the relationship among geography, cultural dislocation, and survival by juxtaposing First and Third World communities in *Daughters*.

Gender, race, and class comprise a dynamic that is often underestimated in its power to perpetuate psychic fracturing. Chapter 3 analyzes the workings of these forces in Marshall's fiction. The alienated men in *Soul Clap Hands and Sing* function as early examples of different kinds of fracturing and the subsequent failure of survival. One section identifies selected images of capitalism and discusses the threat posed to the psyche in the world of work. Merle Kinbona's psychic stabilization through the culturally rich practice of talk, an art in black communities, revealingly counters the failed men of *Soul Clap Hands*. Situating Merle's recovery in a community-based behavior is an important precursor to the role of community and heritage in achieving spiritual wholeness.

Chapter 4 explores the attaining of spiritual wholeness in *Praisesong*, the culmination of a particular vision that compelled Marshall's fiction beginning in the mid-1950s. The first section compares her development of materialism and labor with that of other black women writers who have depicted the destructiveness of materialism and of race, gender, and class but have not envisioned a means of salvaging the fractured psyche. The chapter also analyzes the role of elders or ancestors—Aunt Cuney and Lebert Joseph in *Praisesong*, Miss Thompson in *Brown Girl*, and Leesy in *The Chosen Place*—exponents of psychic wholeness in Marshall's fiction. Spiritual wholeness may replace fracturing when the character reclaims self from the killing impulses of capitalism-materialism and consciously participates in redefining them; when suspicion and misplaced ethnocentrism among displaced people of African descent are replaced by the acknowledgment of cultural connectedness, regardless of physical domicile; and when myth and ritual become privileged rather than suspect.

The last chapter focuses on Marshall's most recent novel, *Daughters*. This chapter continues a discussion begun in chapter 2 in which black male and female partnership is posited as essential to salvaging and preserving the community. Sons of the community are tractable in Caribbean neocolonialist and American postslavery games of political domination. Daughters are more likely to have attained spirituality and are also more likely to return their service to the community. Several female characters in *Daughters* demonstrate characteristics of wholeness and thus move beyond its quest. This chapter analyzes their involvement in community and their personal lives in light of that accomplishment.

 CHAPTER ONE

Generative Spaces: Paule Marshall's Imaginative Vision

> With the exception of Lorraine Hansberry, black women writers remained obscure and unread during the decades dominated by civil rights and black nationalism. —Mary Helen Washington

Naming the Phenomenon

In 1959, when Paule Marshall's first novel, *Brown Girl, Brownstones*, was published, Rosa Parks had defied tradition and authority in Montgomery, Alabama, by refusing to relinquish her seat on a public bus and thus initiated the civil rights movement. But the excavation of black literary texts that had been forgotten, dismissed, or ignored remained in the future. The literary scholars and critics who would assume the work on a scale heretofore unexperienced in African-American writing were, in many cases, too young to envision what their careers would become. The women's movement and its offsprings of feminism and feminist literary criticism were amorphous shapes awaiting the definition that would follow in the wake of the civil rights movement. Neither black literary critics nor readers were anxiously awaiting the publication of new fiction by black women. No gynocritics waited to assess Marshall's new novel, to interpret its responsiveness to a tradition of black women's literature, to determine whether it transcended tradition, or to ascertain whether the resonance of Marshall's voice could redirect a literary chorus of both male and female voices.[1]

Not until late in the 1980s, after nearly two decades of sustained publishing by African-American women, could a community of writers authoritatively be conceptualized. Not until that decade would Hortense Spillers declare that "the community of Black women writing in the United States now can be regarded as a vivid new fact of national life" ("Cross-Currents," 249). The accuracy of Spillers's assessment is evident not only in the amount of fiction published since 1970 but also in the national acclaim and sales records of fiction by African-American women.[2] Of course, a tradition of black women's fiction existed when *Brown Girl, Brownstones* appeared, but women writers neither claimed nor expected national readership. They had little if any conscious feeling of being part of a group of writers or of being directed by gender and culture. Perhaps more important, they had not yet experienced the turbulent, radicalizing 1960s, the decade that would galvanize ideologies and reorder literary representations of black life and culture, particularly the depiction of black women's lives.

Without cohesive impulses shaping black women's writing in the fifties and sixties, comparative relationships between Marshall's fiction and that of her contemporaries are important for what they reveal about the vision that unifies Marshall's work. *Brown Girl* signals its discreteness in several ways—through depicting the assimilation efforts of immigrant Afro-Caribbeans and their tentative failures and successes with materialism in the American capitalist system; through balanced characterizations of black males and females; through the complex rendering of Silla Boyce as wife, mother, and materialist; and finally through its simultaneous attention to a girl's coming-of-age and her recognition of cultural displacement.[3]

What sets Marshall's vision apart is her perception of the consequences of cultural displacement for people of African descent, consequences that may significantly exacerbate the oppressions of gender,

race, and class. Other writers' imaginations in general embrace survival and chronicle defeat in a racist society. Marshall adds considerations of gender and class to what happens to her characters. Moreover, she contrasts physical and material survival in Eurocentric spaces
with spiritual affirmation that can be acquired through cultural embrace and connection. She links problems such as identity, insecurity,
and spiritual malaise to psychic fragmentation and moves toward acquiring wholeness through identification with African origins. Thus, a
consistent strand in Marshall's fiction up to *Daughters* (1991)—*Brown
Girl, Brownstones, Soul Clap Hands and Sing* (1961), *The Chosen Place,
The Timeless People* (1969), *Praisesong for the Widow* (1983), *Reena and
Other Stories* (1983)—is the exploration and systematic exposure of the
fractured psyche of people of African descent.

Marshall's fiction offers a cogent conception of people of African
descent. The unity of her writing distinguishes it from that of other
writers. She writes with grace and perception and with recognition of
the special history that has continued to exercise a vital role in the
lives of African Americans.[4] In re-creating experiences of the African
diaspora population, Marshall's corpus constitutes an artful, original,
and sustained presentation of the causes and effects of a fractured psyche. As important, her fiction demonstrates how self healing may be
generated within the black cultural matrix.

Fractured means broken, splintered, or ruptured; in the traditional
literary sense, *psyche* refers to the invisible soul that complements the
physical body, a presence rooted in myth but validated through psychology. Thus, a fractured psyche affects identity and threatens psychic
survival unless it is repaired. Joseph A. Baldwin's research emphasizes the necessity of understanding an "African psyche . . . to explain
the obvious aberration in it to account for the current self-destructive
predicament of African American mental health" ("African Self Consciousness," 179). He investigates the disparity between the American
black psyche and its African component using the negative influence
of Western reality and demonstrates the need for a racial-cultural consciousness with African origins. This position meshes with the ideas of
Marshall's fiction.

Fracturing may be attributed to adaptation and survival in the hostile environments encountered by the earliest involuntary African immigrants. Robert Blauner's distinctions between voluntary immigrants and those coming against their will, whom he terms "colonized," offers evidence of a cultural response that makes fracturing the overwhelming result. Africans in America were "overwhelmingly bondsmen" (151), he writes, while those remaining in Africa under British, Portuguese, and Dutch domination at least "helped maintain communities and group life and thus countered the uprooting tendencies and the cultural and psychic penetration of colonialism" (153). Because of their colonized entry, blacks in the United States experienced substantive "historical dislocations" before they could attain economic parity with voluntary immigrants (155).

In writing about the twentieth-century descendants of the colonized, Marshall offers evidence of fracturing as it manifests itself through behavior and attitude. Fracturing disorients perceptions of the world and complicates the manner of survival. The fractured psyche is identifiable (or suspected) through feelings and states of incompleteness, vulnerability, alienation, indirection, displacement, and identity diffusion. It is frequently an insidious condition, partially or wholly disabling or inciting self-destructive behavior that seemingly stems from unfathomable origins if observers' judgments are informed by a Eurocentric perspective.

Specialists in African-American history and behavior recognize the legitimacy of the fractured psyche and its historical antecedents. Saunders Redding cites numerous examples of adaptation to the hostile environments in which slaves found themselves and of the "deep psychic trauma" that affected their behavior (85–88). Na'im Akbar describes the effects of slavery on present lives as the "pain of times past [continuing] to call out from the genetic memories of those whose ancestors survived the test of slavery" (14–15). Therefore, the fractured psyche is problematic and deceptive because the source of its origin has become conveniently categorized as an experience that has been surpassed or exists as an unpleasant memory of history.

Marshall's fiction derives its contours from the history of coerced Africans in the West. Her male characters endure the oppressiveness of race and class, while her female characters contend with the triple jeopardy of gender, race, and class. As characters face a tenuous future, they constantly live with the numbing knowledge of the past as a part of their present. For people of African ancestry, memory decrees that the lessons of history forecast an unstable future. History serves as a powerful record that justifies uncertainty, fear, and outrage, resonating with the trauma of the Middle Passage, of terrible displacement from the familiar, of powerlessness over family, of the violence and displacement of Reconstruction, and of subsequent governmental legitimization of discrimination. The intangible scars of these acts have become the legacy of subsequent generations of African-Americans in spite of the ideology of democratic equality. The conflicts of Marshall's characters— their search for an identity, for fulfilling relationships, and for spiritual wholeness—originate in the perpetuation of oppression. Without writing overt historical fiction frozen in the specificity of an epoch, Marshall has written fiction that is historical because it both recognizes and addresses the influence of the past upon the lives of the present. This distressing weight manifests itself through various postures of severity as black people contend with Western constructions of culture that are antithetical to African sensibility. Anthropologists and psychologists identify the African mental construct as having a "direct, intuitive, and harmonious relation to life and the cosmos . . . different from the cold conceptual logic of European civilization" (Jackson, 246). History as structure and revelation thus becomes an indispensable context for insightful investigation of descendants of Africa.

Marshall's characters clearly carry the burden of the past, as shown by their absence of wholeness as they exist within their communities. Her fiction illustrates, for example, that diminished racial solidarity and impaired cultural identification exemplify behavioral characteristics of the fractured psyche. Fracturing offsets cultural homogeneity in many ways: through intraracial self-distancing, rejection of cultural and or racial identity, indifference to and devaluing of cultural identification, voluntary geographical separatism, concealing or rejecting the personal past, dismissing the historic past, and obsessive and destructive materialism. Before psychological equilibrium becomes possible, these manifestations of fracturing must be confronted and resolved.

Resolution is an evasive quality in most fiction that offers evidence of a fractured psyche. Neither naming the condition nor consistently exploring it, writers of different literary periods, male as well as female, have identified the symptoms of fracturing and illustrated its destructive results. For example, Reena and her brother's desire and attempt to "pass" in Charles Chesnutt's *The House Behind the Cedars* illustrate racial separatism, among other symptoms. Helga Crane and Claire Kendry in Nella Larsen's *Quicksand* and *Passing*, respectively, search for intimacy and acceptance amid racial ambivalence; they owe their maladjustments to a fractured psyche. Similarly, Mrs. Turner's virulent hatred of the African component of her identity in Zora Neale Hurston's *Their Eyes Were Watching God* reflects intraracial distancing and self-rejection. Bigger Thomas in Richard Wright's *Native Son*, Gabriel Grimes in James Baldwin's *Go Tell it on the Mountain*, and Kristin Hunter's outlaw child-woman Rosie in *God Bless the Child* all perceive themselves as outsiders both in their immediate families and in the prevailing culture, and they are similarly affected by the absence of psychological and spiritual wholeness. In Toni Morrison's *The Bluest Eye*, the entire Breedlove family, and especially Pecola, is victimized by the unattainable conceptions of beauty that are idolized by the dominant culture, representing an extreme result of fracturing.

Marshall's distinction from these writers' exploration is her measured movement toward a potential answer, which can be illustrated by an overview of her work. In *Brown Girl, Brownstones*, for example, character and situation demonstrate the presence of a fractured psyche and illustrate many of its consequences. Although scholars view the novel primarily as a bildungsroman, the story of Selina Boyce's turbulent coming-of-age in the household of Barbadian immigrants living in Brooklyn, Marshall effectively maintains a dichotomous focus that is explicit in the title of the book. The story of Selina is equally the story of acquiring the brownstone. Neither story can be told without Silla Boyce, Selina's mother. The parents' accommodation to and seduction by American mores and material values introduce dominant themes of identity blurring, displacement, alienation, and the obscuring or loss of self in the effort to survive, all symptoms of the fractured psyche.

Selina's coming-of-age with its attendant conflicts is complicated through the frictions of her parents and the contrastive behaviors in her community. The irreparable fractured psyches of her father, unmanned in Barbados before he was a man, and of her mother, who restores her dignity after domestic work through language, defer hope for Selina's emergence as a spiritually whole self. But at the end of the novel, having survived initiation rites of sex, race, and gender, she is poised for discovery of the West Indian dimension of her heritage. Possessing two Barbadian bracelets like all her friends, she tosses one of them into the revitalization area of the brownstones, symbolically acknowledging the people and the environment that have contributed to her development. The other bracelet, however, will be worn to Barbados when she travels there to experience her other history. Embracing her cultures bodes positively for the spiritual wholeness of Selina Boyce, although that potential is prefigured rather than developed.

The characterization of other Barbadians as well as an elderly southern woman allows Marshall to illustrate different postures of a fractured psyche. Moreover, the themes, images, motifs, and symbols that engage her attention in *Brown Girl* return in her later fiction.

Soul Clap Hands and Sing, more narrowly conceived than *Brown Girl*, exposes the spiritual emptiness of four aged men in their futile bids at self-revitalization and isolates individual failures and the tragedy of loneliness. Interestingly, the men in these stories turn to women as the source of their renewal, but they have waited too long. Although women's capacity for renewal is not elaborately articulated in this early work, the recognition is crucial, for it foreshadows their potential for exhaustive development in later texts. As important, Marshall employs four geographical areas in these novellas in affirmation of her concept of a worldwide black community beset by similar injuries to the psyche.

Marshall's third novel, *The Chosen Place, the Timeless People* is ambitious in setting, concept, and thematic inclusiveness and is the only one of her works set exclusively in the Caribbean, on a fictional island, Bourne. The setting accommodates the history of British colonialism and the oppressive remnants of postcolonial structures. Marshall depicts an entire community of Bournehills peasants who embody the fractured psyche, with Merle Kinbona featured as the severely fractured female protagonist. Merle's conflicts, the consequence of history and heritage, become the riveting focus of the book. Her salvation lies in claiming ownership of herself and in activating self-healing through the valued art of "talking." Unlike Merle, Vere, another Bournehills native, seeks affirmation of his identity through symbols of Western industrialization rather than through community values, and he fails.

Definitively affirming the origin and perpetuation of the fractured psyche among people of the African diaspora, *The Chosen Place* posits the West in dominion over the Third World, represented by a Caribbean island. Saul and Harriet Amron and British-owned industry represent the West, though Saul's Jewishness considerably mediates his representation. Harriet, however, a twentieth-century link to the slave trade, remains detached from the islanders in spite of their physical proximity, and she fails to recognize how the West functions in oppressing the islanders.

Reena and Other Stories, a collection of disparate pieces, is not a thematically conceived work like *Soul Clap Hands.* But the title story, "Reena," an early work, offers an important view of the author's concern with fracturing. Its encapsulation of the history and problems of black educated urban women of the 1940s and '50s foreshadows Marshall's conception of the forces that impede women's survival.

In *Praisesong for the Widow,* Marshall brings her discussion of the fractured psyche to satisfactory closure. Significantly, many characteristics of Silla and Deighton Boyce reappear in Avatara and Jerome Johnson. Both couples lose the stabilization of self in black culture in their frenzied pursuit of material comforts in a capitalist society, and both men die without learning how they might have survived differently. Silla lives, but she has little recognition of what has happened to her self. Thus, only her daughter, Selina, offers hope for cultural continuity. Avatara in *Praisesong,* however, rediscovers her essential spiritual self by reconnecting with her African cultural origins on a Caribbean island. The displaced African cultural remnants retained through dance, myth, legend, orality, and group names and scattered among all people of the African diaspora resonate in this text. They affirm that the divisiveness of Eurocentric cosmology can be countered through sensitivity to and acceptance of one's cultural origins. The result is a self that is whole and moored.

Praisesong brings full circle the novelist's exploration of the fractured psyche, the regeneration of wholeness, and the proper mental distancing necessary to retain psychological equilibrium. The concluding image in *Brown Girl* is a young woman poised for potential discovery of spiritual wholeness through full knowledge of her heritage. *The Chosen Place* concludes with Merle's regeneration partially completed before she travels to Africa in search of her husband and child. Although potential exists for spiritual restoration in the motherland, that actualization is not a part of the novel. But in *Praisesong*, Avatara Johnson experiences spiritual regeneration in Carriacou, a small, isolated, Caribbean island where remnants of African culture survives in rituals, family names, and dance. The story of Avatara and Jerome Johnson is the consummate American success story of financial achievement and stability as a result of hard work and sacrifice.

Their story shines with the possibilities for any industrious man and woman who plan, budget, and work tirelessly to attain the American dream.[5] After twenty years of perseverance, the Johnsons are able to relocate from the black neighborhood of Halsey Street to surburban White Plains. Jerome owns an accounting business; Avey becomes a leisured homemaker. Silla Boyce's dream, only partially achieved in Marshall's first novel, is brought to fruition in *Praisesong*. Both novels, however, offer a critique of (and a warning about) the perniciousness of materialism and class climbing in displacing the cultural stability of African Americans. Both works explore manifestations of the fractured psyche through the characters' compulsion to identify with ways of being prized within the dominant culture. Both expose the self-distortion that occurs when priorities are displaced in pursuit of materialistic success. In their complete embracing of the dream, characters lose their selves. When they became culturally vacuous and unmoored, they become destructive. For example, in *Brown Girl*, Silla Boyce, motivated by ownership of property, becomes an instrument in her husband's eventual death. Beryl Challenor and Clive, minor characters, become casualties in their parents' rigid strategies for success.

Beryl's self is absorbed by her father's inflexible program for her career in America. Clive's rebellion against his parents' plans for his economic ascent has immobilized him in guilt for disappointing them. Jerome Johnson in *Praisesong* begins repeating racist myths about black men and their disdain for work. Jerome dies without reclaiming himself, but Avey, though initially resistant, confronts what she has lost and becomes self-reaffirmed through intimate reconnection with her cultural roots.

Daughters, Marshall's posttrilogy novel, takes a different direction. Its central conflict, a young woman's disengagement from her father's emotional domination, does not involve a search for psychic reintegration. Moreover, several women in *Daughters* demonstrate the ability to manage the invasion of Western concepts in African-American and Caribbean cultures; these concepts proved a constant source of psychic injury in Marshall's preceding novels. Thus, *Daughters* illustrates characters who have subordinated Western concepts and centered the traditional African cultural worldview. Although the novel engages characters affected by a fractured psyche and the conditions responsible for it, this matter and the achievement of spiritual wholeness are not textually centered.

Although other writers have depicted the consequences of the fractured psyche, Marshall's fiction offers a sustained illustration of the phenomenon, explores the multidimensionality of the problem, and provides a progressive spiral toward solution. Her novels expose the personal, social, and historical conflict that result from assaults on the psyche. Her vision transcends geographical boundaries in its realization of the total black community and encompasses the African diaspora by acknowledging the historical antecedents of this condition. Unlike problem-centered fiction, which offers no solutions or only untenable ones, Marshall's works recommend healing of the spirit and wholeness as viable correctives for the fractured psyche.

Spirituality as a viable component of the psyche is acknowledged in the literature of African-American psychology. Baldwin defines it as "a dynamic energy that allows the self to merge (extend) into the totality of phenomenal experience" ("African Self Consciousness," 180). Linda

James Myers's extensive discussion of the term identifies its crucial position in the African worldview (as distinct from European concepts). It is the "first construct of traditional African philosophical thought, the notion that there is an all pervasive 'energy' that is the source, sustainer, and essence of all phenomenon. . . . Spirit is defined as that pervasive essence that is known in an extrasensory fashion (i.e., the fastest moving energy, consciousness, God)" (75).

As used here, *spirituality* refers to the concept as it exists in the African worldview and not in Western Christian religion. Myers points out that in traditional African culture, the sense of self encompasses time and includes "all of the ancestors, the yet unborn, all of nature, and the entire community" (76). Descendants of Africans in America not only have had their cultural bonds ruptured but also have had their heritage denied or distorted. Marshall, therefore, is insightful and assertive when she positions recovery from spiritual miasma through cultural connections. Recovery of the denigrated and abused self is possible by regenerating the spirit. One beginning is the affirmation of an ancestry that joins black people across barriers of distance, water, and time.

Since the history of displaced Africans is characterized by a powerful negation of motherland Africa and centuries of misinformation, the process of healing is complex. Discerning the myths and distortions that the West has perpetuated about Africa and perceiving them as another guise of subversive oppression becomes a necessary step in this recovery. Establishing connections with the ancestry and culture of one's origin also includes rejecting the doubleness that W. E. B. DuBois acknowledged. Significantly, psychic reintegration largely refers to a mental process of distancing oneself from Western concepts to become receptive to a different nature of reality and to become empowered through it. This process involves recognizing the dialectics of Western concepts and consciously reapportioning them into a system consistent with the philosophical concepts of the displaced culture. This process of holistic restoration, called spiritual reclamation, binds up a fractured psyche.

Marshall's synthesis of the fractured psyche with identification of one's cultural ties to Africa marks her vision as assertively and progressively Afrocentric. Molefi Kete Asante's discussion (168–81) of the necessity for culturally based judgments that take into account the centrality of African ideals and behavior is reflected in Marshall's texts.

Paule Marshall and the Tradition of African American Women Writers

> The Black writer's embattled struggle for fulfillment in America
> [James Baldwin] came to imply, was a recapitulation of the quest
> of all black Americans for expressive wholeness.—Houston Baker

The publication dates of Marshall's fiction distance her from three watershed periods in African-American literary history. *Brown Girl* (1959) appears well after the work of Harlem Renaissance writers and after the naturalistic fiction of the 1940s. *The Chosen Place* (1969) comes at the close of the civil rights decade of the 1960s, characterized by protest literature, but precedes the 1970s, a decade Mary Helen Washington has called the "renaissance of black women writers" ("New Lives," 2). Although the publication date for *Soul Clap Hands and Sing* (1961) situates it within the civil rights decade, the novellas's vision effectively removes them from the overtones of black nationalistic ideology and the social protest that characterizes much of that era's fiction and poetry. *Praisesong*, however, firmly occupies its niche among the black woman–focused fiction published during the 1980s and thus participates in affirming the renaissance begun in the 1970s. A discussion that uses these periods as context and places Marshall's work in contradistinction to them reinforces the emphasis on the unity of her vision even as it affirms her ideological standing in African-American literary tradition and among other women writers. This activity is essential for affirming her consonance within both traditions.

The subject of a women's tradition in African-American literature remains under discussion among some critics. This information is not revolutionary; historically, women's participation in arenas of black life other than writing has been neither sought nor welcomed but rather discouraged. The rejection of women's participation in the early days of the civil rights movement, for example, except in clerical or minor positions supporting black men, is documented (Giddings, 109–17). The practice in African-American politics and literature, prior to the voices of black feminist critics, has been the exclusion or relegation to minor status of all but one or two women. If one definition of tradition is evidence of ongoing enterprise by predecessors whose examples make serviceable models for oncoming generations, then it follows that the body of literature written by black women since the eighteenth century constitutes a tradition.

Documenting the tradition in black women's literature is largely carried on by black feminist scholars engaged in resurrecting out-of-print books and evolving a culturally based critical theory to accommodate the myriad shapes of black fiction. This work assures that women writers (both forgotten and well known) occupy the space they have forged for themselves. In "Toward a Black Feminist Criticism" (1977), Barbara Smith asserts that the feminist critic must "work from the assumption that Black women writers constitute an identifiable literary tradition. . . . Not only is theirs a verifiable historical tradition that parallels in time the tradition of Black men and white women writing in this country, but that thematically, stylistically, aesthetically, and conceptually Black women writers manifest common approaches to the act of creating literature as a direct result of the specific political, social, and economic experience they have been obliged to share" (174).

Mary Helen Washington also confirms a tradition in black women's writing. "Women have worked assiduously in this tradition as writers, as editors, sometimes, though rarely, as critics, and yet every study of Afro-American narrative, every anthology of *the* Afro-American literary tradition has set forth a model of literary paternity in which each male author vies with his predecessor for greater authenticity, greater control over *his* voice, thus fulfilling the mission his *forefathers* left unfinished." [6]

In *The Afro-American Novel and its Tradition*, Bernard Bell cautiously suggests that the differing perspectives of black women novelists do "not necessarily mean that their works constitute a distinctive literary tradition" and enlists statements of black feminists to "underscore the problematics of a separate black female literary tradition" (242–43).[7] In contrast, Stephen Henderson writes in the introduction to *Black Women Writers (1950–1980)* that "one could, in fact, make the case that, the founders of Black American literature, in a formal sense, were women—Phillis Wheatley, Lucy Terry, and Harriet E. Wilson" (xxiii). And Michael Awkward deftly extends Henry Louis Gates, Jr.'s, theory of "chartable formal literary relationships" to study a tradition among black women novelists that he labels "inspiriting influences" (6–8).

A black women's tradition in African-American literature is verifiable through the continuum of women's writing. An evolving critical methodology that develops original modes of discovery of intertextual relationships will illuminate these previously obscure connections. The strongest and most consistent continuity within the tradition, as Washington has recognized, is the black woman's story in all its myriad configurations (*Black-Eyed Susans*, x). Marshall is not only an integral part of that tradition but also a lodestar within it. Her precise prose, the tight structures of her novels, and the chiseled complexity of her characters more than sufficiently anchor her in the tradition. Moreover, the accolades accorded Marshall by scholar/critics and other creative writers bespeak the recognition of her importance within both a black women's separate tradition and African-American literature. Spillers, for example, cites Marshall, Toni Morrison, and Toni Cade Bambara as writers who participate "in a tradition of black women writing in their own behalf, close to its moment of inception" ("A Hateful Passion," 185). Charles Johnson notes Marshall's "steady production of first-rate writing and a spiritual balance and emotional maturity rare in much black fiction" (100). Johnson also credits *Brown Girl's* innovation in dramatizing a youngster's vacillation between two extremes represented by parents: As "fruitful as this situation has been in recent black fiction, Paule Marshall is the writer who got there first" (101). In "Zora Neale Hurston: A Cautionary Tale and A Partisan View," Alice Walker refers to Marshall as "unequaled in intelligence, vision, craft by anyone of her generation, to put her contributions to our literature modestly" (84).

Aside from the accolades, it is essential and revealing to read Marshall's fiction in relation to fictional models by black women writers during the three watershed periods previously mentioned. To do so, her works must be seen as vital participants in black women's literary tradition. Her corpus is immeasurably significant to the tradition, for not only has Marshall worked within it, but she has also provided a redirective component. With the publication of *Praisesong* and its means for healing the fractured psyche and reclaiming spirituality, a serviceable model has been added to the tradition. It is a model that resonates with black women's fiction of the 1980s, in which there is a sense of nurturing connectiveness among black women and a sense of spiritual homecoming. *Daughters* illustrates that Marshall reached closure to her vision of spiritual healing and with subsequent fiction will explore other trajectories.

Marshall's fiction, although chronologically and thematically removed from the three major eras of black writing, nevertheless reflects identifiable characteristics of the tradition that connects Nella Larsen's *Quicksand* and Jessie Fauset's *Plum Bun* (emblematic of the content and indicative of the aspirations for black women in the 1920s), Hurston's *Their Eyes Were Watching God* (which signals different interpretive stances for the 1930s), and Ann Petry's *The Street* (representing black female response to the naturalism of the 1940s). Black women's literary tradition therefore includes multiple ways of interpreting existence for black women in a society that defines them narrowly—if it chooses to make them visible at all. It follows, then, that black women's responses have largely reacted to exterior stimuli. This rationale applies to the mulatto presence in Larsen and Fauset as well as to their predecessors Pauline Hopkins and Frances Ellen Watkins Harper. Women characters as heirs to the "racial uplift" ideology of the 1890s as well as the 1920s seek acculturation into American society on an equal footing with Anglo-Americans through educational attainment and physical appearance. Fauset and Larsen promote Euro-American female beauty—fair skin, straight hair, thin facial features, style, and poise—as essential to economic and social status for black women. Fauset's and Larsen's practice of affirming their protagonists' humanity through a concept of physical beauty merely confirms the persistent (but unfortunate) link between skin color and human worth. In a society that disempowers women, they seek to access power, authority, and material goods through marriage. These concerns envelope women's lives in Fauset and Larsen and are integral to the fiction of their successors.

Black women's means of attaining power, authority, and material goods in the continuum of black women's writing offers one juncture for discussion of tradition. Might an intertextually disjunctive relationship be charted through analysis of how these subjects shape texts and black women's lives as marginalized and Other? Accessing power, authority, and material goods subsumes individuation in Fauset and Larsen; individuation subsumes these things, however, in Hurston's *Their Eyes Were Watching God*, a text that "create[s] so sharp a rift on the literary surface that from the angle even of the late thirties, Larsen and Fauset have already become signs of a reliquary" (Spillers, "Cross-Currents," 252).

Although Janie Crawford in *Their Eyes* is deemed a beautiful woman, exhibiting the physical attributes of a mulatto, physical features neither dominate the text nor determine Janie's responses to people. References to Janie's appearance, in fact, may be interpreted as a subtle critique of the dominance of beauty in black female fictive discourse. More obviously, Hurston critiques the debilitating isolation of middle-class existence during Janie's years with Jody Starks. Janie achieves the ambitions that animate the women of Fauset and Larsen: she acquires a husband who has wrested power, invested himself with authority, and enabled himself materially. Her benefits from sharing in his accomplishments, however, stymie her development and cause psychic division. Hurston's exposé of the artificiality of this queenlike position questions the value of satisfying a woman's ambitions through means that are not self-generated. Janie's rejection of material possessions and social status during her marriage to Tea Cake are stunning reversals of the desires that shaped women's lives in preceding texts. As important, the closure of black women's texts offers insightful conclusions in resolving tensions among power, authority, and material goods. Janie achieves unquestionable autonomy, for example, only when she is manless, thus confirming that whatever power and authority she owns are independent of male origination or support. As numerous critics have pointed out, Janie has acquired the power of voice rooted in cultural expression and thus the authority to name her own experiences.

Ann Petry's *The Street* (1946) resonates with previously published texts in its delineation of a female protagonist in quest of power and authority. Petry's novel, traditionally grouped with the naturalistic fiction of Richard Wright's stamp, should be examined for significant strains that speak to a tradition in black women's fiction. The novel may appropriately be read as a variation in critiquing the process of access to power, authority, and materialism. The linear structure of Lutie Johnson's ineffectual scrimmages with 116th Street in Harlem—with its self perpetuating cycle of poverty, crime, and social problems—complements Lutie's successive attempts to wrest power and authority through effort. After she observes the wealth of a white family where she works as a live-in maid for a year and listens to the Protestant work ethic that they espouse and that their money confirms, Lutie determines that she is capable by her own industry and desire of translating effort into financial success. Thus, Petry depicts an ambitious, working-class black woman who ignores gender, race, and class oppressions only to become defeated by them. Bernard Bell's conclusions that Petry "effectively debunks the myths of urban success and progress, of rural innocence and virtue, and of pathological black women and men" in writing about the black community and that she cuts her protagonists "from a different cloth than those of her major contemporaries" (Himes and Wright), although accurate, emphasize only one dimension of the text ("Ann Petry's Demythologizing," 106, 114). *The Street* brings the white world of privilege and power into comparative proximity with the black community through Lutie, a sojourner in both. Lutie's economic determinism centralizes the ideology of the American dream as she immerses herself in its realization and experiences its failure. Primary in *The Street* is a black female quest for self-empowerment, authority in her own right (not through male intervention), and material gain through the process that supposedly is available to any able-bodied American citizen. Lutie Johnson fails not only because of the defeatism of the environment of 116th street but also because of the liabilities of race, gender, and class, all of which are intricately connected forces that Petry apparently understands. Significantly, Lutie operates in isolation from a communal base, family, and female friendships, all of which in some degree inform Janie Crawford's success in *Their Eyes*.

Marshall has discussed Gwendolyn Brooks's *Maud Martha* (1953) as the work from the 1950s that offers a model for her own thinking about depicting black women in fiction (Pettis). Brooks's character brings to women's fiction the interior vantage point of a female protagonist reacting to her devaluation both within and outside of the African-American community. This response can be attributed to each community's hierarchical valuing of superficial physical beauty. Maud Martha's marriage fails to invest her with the useless power of being a wife in the community, and no source exists from which Maud might accrue power or authority. Maud's depiction as a black woman grappling with self-esteem and psychic survival because of her skin color raises an issue in fiction that had not received sustained treatment and thereby brings an additional dimension to the tradition of black women's writing.

Marshall's fiction resonates with other black women's writings. Black women are central to her novels and short fiction, even where black males dominate, as in *Soul Clap Hands and Sing*. Her corpus delineates the multiple ways in which black women (and men) seek out ways of surviving, even thriving, in environments antithetical to their having or exercising power and authority. In many characters, *Brown Girl* in particular critiques materialism run amok in the pursuit of the American dream and the emotional trauma that it may cause.

In discussing a tradition in black women's writing, the centrality of the black female to the family unit in the continuity of African-American generations is apparent, as is the dialectic between black women's immersion in family structure and their autonomy separate from family. Moreover, the refutation of stereotypical images imposed on the population generally and those levied specifically against women constitutes a dimension of the tradition. In *Brown Girl*, to cite one of numerous examples, Silla Boyce debunks the stereotype of the monolithic, strong, black woman through Marshall's adroit merging and conflicting of physical strength and emotional weakness. Silla, capable of inclusive love, is equally capable of incoercible hate. She is a realist, conversant with the culture from which she immigrated as well as with the requirements of satisfying her materialist goals in New York. In the minor character Suggie, Marshall's flirtation with the stereotype of the loose woman coalesces with a multidimensional woman whose sexuality helps her mediate class-oriented responses. Suggie's need for male companionship actually abets her psychological well-being instead of diminishing her capacity for self-respect.

Increasing attention to female culture and friendship as nurturing and sustaining black women merits the inclusion of this subject in a discussion of tradition. In fiction written since the 1970s, a relationship often exists between the absence of a supportive female community and a woman's success in either problem solving or self-definition. *Brown Girl* precedes Morrison's *Sula* and Walker's *The Color Purple* in its delineation of a vibrant female culture and friendship between women as essential to survival in hostile communities. Through talk, social activities, and mutual support, Silla Boyce and her transplanted immigrant friends share injustices and reclaim the dignity of womanhood. In addition, the friendship between Selina Boyce and Beryl Challenor is essential to the pain and awkwardness of their preadolescent years. Perhaps it even cushions Selina's temporary dislocations as she comes of age in an adult world.

When recurring subjects in black women's fiction are studied, they disclose, among other features, attention to realities for African-American people surrounded by Euro-American values; consistent vision in the results of race, class, and gender; multiple ways of delineating black women; separation of myths from realities; cultural and social differences in empowering blacks; and psychic divisions of the kind articulated by DuBois as the result of living simultaneously in two cultures. Marshall's fiction expands these recurring subjects through its inclusion of the cultural experience of peoples of the African diaspora.

Barbara Christian's observation that Marshall has formed "a unique vision or philosophy of life in her creation of her world" in representing "distinct trends in American literature" recognizes this recurrence in Marshall's corpus (*Black Women Novelists*, 79). In its exploration of ongoing consequences of physical dispersal and spiritual rootlessness, Marshall's work promotes the view that true spiritual ease can occur only when displaced descendants psychologically accept and embrace the culture of their origin.

The endings of Marshall's novels offer the strongest evidence for this reading. Selina Boyce in *Brown Girl* stands poised for a journey to Barbados, a destination that reflects her inclination to accept and to learn about her parents' cultural heritage. At the end of *The Chosen Place*, on the fictional Bourne Island, Merle Kinbona has reconciled antithetical Afro-Caribbean and colonial British heritages that fought within her. Her destination is Africa, which, although not offered as a panacea, has the unmistakable potential for providing spiritual ease. *Praisesong* completes the implication of these earlier journeys by bringing together the connected cultural practices of West Africa, the black American South, and the Caribbean. It is Marshall's strongest evidence for placing spiritual reclamation and healing within the black cultural matrix. These facets of Marshall's fiction, as well as the manner in which her corpus resonates within the tradition of black women's literature, assure her permanence within it.

Literary and Biographical Connections

> A survey of Caribbean literature and the scholarship it generates
> indicates that . . . the Caribbean literary imagination is shaped
> essentially by the two major forces of colonialism and
> postcolonialism . . . whether [the people] remained in the region
> or emigrated to England and North America.
>
> —Carol P. Marsh-Lockett

That Marshall sees cultural continuity among black people as an essential component of their wholeness originates in her background as the American-born daughter of West Indians. Her parents immigrated from Barbados to Brooklyn after World War I, her father entering illegally by way of Cuba, where he had gone as a worker on a government scheme (Pettis). Many of the details in Marshall's fiction (particularly in *Brown Girl* and *Daughters*) resonate biographically with the author's experience. Marshall talks candidly about personal mishaps and incidents that are translated into her work, though she cautions that the material is "always altered, is always transformed; it's always reordered to fit the fictional reality" (Dance, 3). Like Marshall, Selina Boyce, for instance, encompasses three cultures—the Afro-Caribbean household of her parents, African-American culture in the schools, and American culture in general. For Marshall, the alienation among the cultures was palpable. Both African-American and Afro-Caribbean groups felt the racism of the dominant culture and reacted, the Afro-Caribbeans by distancing themselves from other blacks, especially southerners, and the African-Americans by accepting stereotypes of the industrious West Indians. Neither group apparently perceived such divisiveness as a self-defeating enterprise among the marginalized.

The West Indian culture that was part of Marshall's daily existence both in Brooklyn and in Barbados, where her mother took her to visit, is invaluable to her fictive vision. Her sense of the Caribbean as a physical place as well as a state of mind and her impression of female ancestors may be traced to visiting Barbados as a young child. Marshall's mother, in spite of her father's objection, took her "home," "to Barbados or

Bimshire, as they affectionately called it, [to] the little Caribbean island in the sun they loved but had to leave. 'Poor—poor but sweet' was the way they remembered it" (Marshall, *Reena and Other Stories*, 25). Marshall and her mother remained there two years, and the youngster was enrolled in the local school, where the British system dominated.

Marshall was heavily influenced by the physical beauty of the place, by the sugarcane that grew plentifully enough to cover the world (Pettis). In "To Da-Duh in Memoriam" (*Reena and Other Stories*, 93–107) the natural beauty of Barbados and Da-Duh's reverential pride in pointing it out to a New York child become the underpinnings of the author's fictional Caribbean islands. The topography of Barbados left indelible etchings, impressions that transmute into defined, whole fictional islands in *The Chosen Place* (Bourne) and *Daughters* (Triunion). The author's evocation of place and reconstruction of cultural landscape is consistent with this pattern in writers with a Caribbean connection, according to Carol Boyce Davies (60).

Long after that childhood visit to Barbados, Marshall's political sense would respond to the patent exploitation of the Third World by the West. The residues of enslavement and of colonialism in *The Chosen Place*, for example, are offered with the perspective of an insider who understands the interplay between power and labor. The stoic dignity of the sugarcane workers is vividly represented in *The Chosen Place* (159–63). The artist's sense of inquiry would seek an explanation for the West Indian peasants' contrariety—their resistance to self-help schemes offered by Western governments and philanthrophic groups. The artist would understand the peasants' gritty survival in spite of spirit-crushing conditions and would perceive that one source of opposition stemmed from a legacy of armed resistance to political invasion. In both *The Chosen Place* and *Daughters*, the inspiration for rejecting outsiders' philanthrophic assistance schemes derives from the veneration of Afro-Caribbean heroes and heroines and the apparent belief that salvation will again emerge from within their own ranks. Until then, the peasants will wait.

The author's child sense marveled at Da-Duh, an old woman who had weathered and tempered with time and taken care of business meanwhile. Marshall's artist sense would transmute that venerable person into the sagacious ancestors so essential to the new generations in her fiction, including Miss Thompson in *Brown Girl*, Leesy Walkes and Carrington in *The Chosen Place*, Medford in "British Guiana" (one of the novellas in *Soul Clap Hands and Sing*), Aunt Cuny and Lebert Joseph in *Praisesong*, and Celestine in *Daughters*.

In a brief introduction to "To Da-Duh, in Memoriam," Marshall refers to the story as "the most autobiographical . . . a reminiscence largely of a visit I paid to my grandmother" (95). But the recollection and shaping of the encounter are also artistic: "I wanted the basic theme of youth and old age to suggest rivalries, dichotomies of a cultural and political nature, having to do with the relationship of western civilization and the Third World" (95). Marshall chose mechanization to dramatize the often destructive power of the West and its nearly inconsequential regard of human beings. The impersonalized bulk and mass of machinery—its ability to impair, maim, or kill human beings—perceived as emblematic of ruthless and powerful nations in their relationships with small Caribbean islands, would forcibly make her statement. Therefore, in Brooklyn in *Brown Girl* the machines are in the factory where Silla and Deighton Boyce, respectively, work; in *The Chosen Place*, they exist in the British-owned sugar processing plant called Cane Vale, situated in Bournehills; and Vere purchases a machine, an Opel automobile made of parts manufactured in Germany and the United States. In "To Da-Duh," the skyscraper and the airplane convey the might of the superpowers.

As a child, the author also listened to her mother talking with her Caribbean friends in the kitchen of their Brooklyn brownstone, and she valued and retained the subtleties and nuances of spoken language. Marshall has reproduced them in her fiction.

In Marshall's reconstruction of black American and Afro-Caribbean culture, women's discourse becomes layered with meaning and significance. Having designated the talkers of the Brooklyn brownstone as poets and teachers in the crafting of dialogue, Marshall writes of conversation as their means of reinvesting themselves with dignity and of again empowering themselves as women after the days of thankless labor as domestics, the only work available to them until factories accepted black women workers during World War II. In "From the Poets in the Kitchen" Marshall praises the use of words and stunning expressions that exercised a power of their own and that motivated her to aspire to its reproduction (11–12). Transferring this scene from memory to fiction, she lovingly reinscribes an interior community of working-class women and places them in the kitchen of Silla Boyce in *Brown Girl*. Interestingly, Marshall satirically counterpoints their meaningful talk in the vacuous reception chatter of middle-class women in *The Chosen Place*. In Merle Kinbona, however, Marshall explores the value of discourse in an extension of abnormal and effusive talk as an artifice, temporarily salvaging total spiritual disintegration.

Marshall's inclusion of the West Indian experience in her major novels is considered justification for her bibliographic inclusion among anglophone Caribbean writers just as her delineation of the African-American experience necessitates her inclusion in bibliographies of black American writers.[8] Writing about the West Indian novel generally and *Chosen Place* specifically, Edward Brathwaite astutely negotiates between the writer's two communities: "Had Paule Marshall been a West Indian, she probably would not have written this book. Had she not been an Afro-American of West Indian parentage, she possibly could not have written it either; for in it we find a West Indies facing the metropolitan West on the one hand, and clinging to a memorial past on the other" ("West Indian History," 226). Thus, Marshall is claimed by the two cultures that she worked to synthesize within herself and to which she lays claim: "I am Afro-Caribbean and Afro-American," she says. "I am embracing both these cultures and I hope that my work reflects what I see as a common bond" (Sandi Russell, 15).

Marshall's sense of her triple identity elevates identity as a major issue in her fiction. In *Brown Girl*, Selina's fragile adolescent self—immersed in Caribbean culture within the family's rented brownstone but exposed, also, to the dominant culture (as represented by the furniture of former inhabitants and Miss Mary) and to African-American culture in the community—must be separated out of the morass so that her identity may be known to herself. Selina's friends, Beryl and Clive, become casualities in their respective parents' efforts to direct their identities. Gerald Motley in "British Guiana" has allowed his triple racial heritage to perpetuate self-division. In *The Chosen Place*, Merle Kinbona must reconcile multiple cultural heritages, including West Indian and British, before her life can move forward constructively. Vere, a minor male character, equates his identity as a man with the successful resurrection of a racing car whose power he vicariously usurps. *Praisesong* addresses Avatara Johnson's identity as determined by the dominant culture as the source of her spiritual moribundity.

Marshall's concern with identity bespeaks her recognition of its importance in black lives, a perception supported by the dominance of this subject in other fiction by black people. Carol Boyce Davies, for example, acknowledges identity as a recurrent characteristic in Afro-Caribbean literary production (60). Similarly, Henry Louis Gates, Jr., has written that "the single most pervasive and consistent assumption of all black writing since the eighteenth century has been that there exists an unassailable, integral, black self, as compelling and as whole in Africa as in the New world, in slavery as without slavery. What's more, this self was *knowable*, retrievable, [and] recuperable" ("Frederick Douglass," 604). Marshall's attention to identity and self in her fiction, which spans five decades, authoritatively affirms her conviction that the self is indeed knowable, retrievable, and recuperable. Marshall's characters' search for self and the healing of a fractured psyche never involves rejection of heritage; rather, the search produces a satisfactory synthesis of the best and most positive assets where multiple heritages are an issue.

Marshall's personal synthesis of Afro-Caribbean and African-American heritages is thus crucial to her vantage point of interconnecting yet disparate cultures. Out of her confidence that synthesis is ideal has emerged her belief that self-identity must ultimately be grounded in acceptance of Africa. Her embracing of cultural continuity and of a spiritual return to Africa is a significant bond among black American women's texts. Although the texts of black women in general aim to expose, explore, and respond to problems and conflicts that impede the lives of black people, especially women, they rarely actively engage the historical dimensions of certain problems.[9] Their vision, circumscribed by race, gender, and class concerns within the United States, has failed to link the problems of black Americans with the problems of other blacks of the African diaspora. Marshall's major fiction, in contrast, constitutes a successive working out of falsely divisive cultural signs; each of Marshall's first three novels, which she rightly conceives as a trilogy, concludes with the protagonist undertaking both a physical and spiritual journey that moves her closer to the destination that will dissolve petty cultural differences because it will affirm acceptance of the spiritual origin of the African diaspora. Marshall's vision, with liberty to transcend black culture within the United States, thus enriches and distinguishes her fiction. Her intimacy with three cultures and her imaginative visioning invites her criticism and questioning of them all.

CHAPTER TWO

An Absence of Wholeness: Negotiating Community in the Strategy of Survival

> Bournehills scarcely seemed a physical place to her, but some
> mysterious and obscured region of the mind which ordinary
> consciousness did not dare admit to light.
>
> —*The Chosen Place, The Timeless People*

Physical Places, Psychological Spaces

The titles of Paule Marshall's first two novels suggest overt bonding between place and people: the brown girl is linked with the brownstones, and the timeless people are wed to the chosen place, a fictional Caribbean community called Bournehills. The titles of the novellas in *Soul Clap Hands and Sing*—"Barbados," "Brooklyn," "British Guiana," and "Brazil"—repeat geographical locations. Although the titles *Praisesong for the Widow* and *Daughters* omit geographical specificity, place and community are nonetheless vital. In the story of protagonist Avatara Johnson in *Praisesong*, Ibo Landing in South Carolina, Halsey Street in New York, and the islands Grenada and Carriacou in the Caribbean all are integral to the stages of her experiences. In *Daughters*, the juxtaposition of communities in the Caribbean and in New York and New Jersey confirm similar qualities in places an ocean apart. Communities in Marshall's fiction embody and reflect the heritage, fortitude, and values that sustain descendants of Africans, but these places simultaneously entail the defeats that derail psyches.

Marshall imposes the idea of community as an entity whose benign or hostile nature should be acknowledged as a viable force in the negotiation of her characters' lives. Psychological space must be separated from physical places where antagonism filters in. If the physical place is a black community, that fact does not make it immune to forces that splinter the psyche.[1] Thus, the necessity for psychological space remains constant for people who have the historical precedents of disruption, removal, and resettlement. Slaves in the Caribbean and in the United States fled to isolated hills to form maroon societies.[2] The U.S. slave community was regularly traumatized by the sale of its members. Willful or forced migration during the post–Civil War years resulted in the disbanding of slave-quarter communities and the evolution of stable communities with self-created structure. But these psychological spaces were not immune to the fracturing ideology of the dominant culture because they could be penetrated by the dominant culture and its ethnocentricism. The great migration northward by the southern black population before World War I marks another stage of community impairment followed by resettlement amid potential hostility. Communities in the Caribbean were disrupted by migration to Great Britain or to urban areas in the United States. Historically, black communities, except for the most geographically isolated ones, have been characterized by shifting populations and subjected to invasion by racially caustic outsiders or their ideology. Given this historical onus, community in the experience of black people is a vital unit in the preservation of a healthy psyche or in healing a fractured one. Therefore, in fiction, community or physical place is often painstakingly developed as an entity important to a character's psychological or physical solace.[3]

In sociological studies, one definition of community encompasses merely the physical place where one lives. In literature, this minimalist definition must always be broadened to include larger concepts of community such as social identification and interaction among inhabitants, thereby inviting thought about how black community and the idea of negotation inform Marshall's fiction. The wider definition also invites consideration of the theoretical relations between individual and community. Dennis Poplin's discussion of the "psychocultural" dimension of community encompasses characteristics that distinguish the black community as a group united by a historical precedent that transcends physical place. The historical milieu from which common values, beliefs, and goals are born fosters community. The "value orientations [pertain] to people's relationship to nature, to the supernatural, [and] to time." Thinking of "we" rather than "they" becomes an identifying quality alongside psychological security and stability (19).

"Negotiation of community" means the character's subliminal agreement to psychological entities such as security, group kinship, and shared values. These phenomena form a supportive web for the enhancement of psychic health that is necessary for meaningful survival. During short-term confrontations or long-term assaults on the psyche, an adept negotiator preserves the self through that group kinship and by drawing from communal strength both literally and metaphorically. As important, negotiation demands distancing, securing the self through consciously framed interiorization. Negotiation urges resistance and adaptation. Marshall's fiction supports a wide gulf between the physical and psychological dimensions of community. The psychological space constitutes the character's intuitive knowledge of mutual origins, common history, shared oppression, and psychic fragility. Although claiming a supportive haven is useful, such space offers, at best, only momentary respite from psychic assault; it provides no guarantee of wholeness. Psychological space may be garnered from physical space that does not contribute to psychic wholeness.

Metaphorical and physical spaces, Melvin Dixon writes, offer the opportunity for "rootedness for both author and protagonist." Dixon believes that geography and identity, closely bonded in African-American literary tradition, can be traced to the homelessness and alienation of African-American writers (2–3). Marshall's work participates in this tradition by exploring relationships between identities and geography, as exemplified, for example, in the identity vacillation of Deighton Boyce in *Brown Girl*; in the equivalence between character and place for Gerald Motley in "British Guiana"; and in Merle Kinbona in Bournehills (*The Chosen Place*). Marshall's fiction provides rootedness to some degree, because identity is often an issue for the fractured psyche and identity is connected to one's community. For example, Motley and Kinbona distinctly embody their communities. They encompass the bleakness of their respective places and topographical ravages. Motley does not perceive that a psychological space in Guiana could offer temporary stasis. Kinbona, fortunately, draws sustenance from her community in working to bind her fractured self. Marshall's fiction offers an intriguing interplay between physical place and psychological space in the negotiation of community.

"To Da-Duh, in Memoriam," a story about a young child from New York visiting her mother's birthplace in the Caribbean, contains the paradigm by which communities may be assessed for their role in salvaging the psyche. The dialectic between rural and urban that surfaces in several of Marshall's works holds significant meaning for psychic sustenance. In this story the experiences and values of a ten-year-old urban child are placed in opposition to those of her elderly island grandmother, Da-Duh. The child already values products of the Western industrial community over the natural properties that Da-Duh cherishes. The child offers contemporary songs learned from the production of vinyl discs and disseminated over radio waves and reveres the height of the Empire State Building, a testament to awesome technological power. Da-Duh's allegiance is tied to the land's natural production— the size of sugarcane in her fields, the profusion of fruit trees that grow in Barbados (guava, breadfruit, mango, sugar apple, lime, and banana).

Although she is impressed by the description of snow, a natural phenomenon alien to her island experience, she nevertheless believes that the city, and by implication, the child's community, is a sterile place: "Nothing can bear there," she says (101). Da-Duh's rigid beliefs reflect the "antinomy of stability and change" in considering community. Change, represented by the industrial force of the West, operates to the detriment of rural, agricultural villages and "indicates their obsolescence" (Minar and Greer, x–xi). In the congenial combativeness between the old island woman and the New York youngster, the child gains the edge in their rivalry when she boasts that the city has a building far taller than a hill or a royal palm tree on the island.

After the child has returned home, England sends its industrial marvel—fighter planes—flying low over the island in an extravaganza of military ego. When they pass, Da-Duh lies dead at the window from which she had watched them, her cane flattened in their wake. Their power foreshadows the destructive ability of technology and prefigures the spiritual demise of Da-Duh's descendants, mesmerized by the capitalistic glamour of alien and hostile communities. But Da-Duh's death is also that of someone who refuses to negotiate for spiritual survival in the face of antagonistic and intrusive forces.[4] For her descendants, inured to a technologically progressive world that influences them to reject land-based values more amenable to the integrity of their spiritual selves, the future is bleak but not impossible.

If Da-duh has the ability to know the future, as many of Marshall's elderly characters do, then she understands that the planes foreshadow the encroachment of technological evolution in countries termed developing. She can see the various deaths, including that of the natural vegetation, that will follow progress. The last scene of the story shows the grown-up granddaughter painting seas of swirling sugarcane in a rented loft in New York City while the vibration of machinery below mocks her efforts. Her gesture of memory to Da-Duh, abysmally futile, nevertheless pays obeisance to the values of Da-duh's natural community. The antithesis between swirling sugarcane and the sound of machinery is despair. The urban, industrial community, handmaiden to capitalism, remains hostile to black people without their conscious negotiation of psychological space, but rural communities with histories of oppression also demand similar negotiation.[5]

In *Praisesong*, another New York child is yearly summoned to the South Carolina sea island of Tatem, "down South," where a great-aunt, unlike Da-Duh, instills the lesson of conscious negotiation, of a necessary separation between the body's physical place and its psychological space. The story of the Ibos' return to Africa by walking across an ocean because their prescient capabilities told them that the New World would be unendurably hostile encodes the paradigm of distance between physical place and psychological space.[6]

The attention given to communication between elderly women (the ancestors in Marshall's fiction) and young girls suggests that aware-ness of psychological space must be taught early if it is to be effective in preventing fracturing. The teaching method relies on indirection, however. The discrete manifestations of a transported heritage that is imparted to young girls are essential in the formation of self and in the definition of community. In Tatem, for example, African wood carving, the ring shout (a transplanted West African dance), and herbal reme-dies are vestiges of a legacy that communicates traditions in art and healing. In *Daughters*, Estelle takes her child, Ursa, to the monument commemorating leaders who resisted slavery. The self-worth that may be generated as a result of knowing about one's indigenous culture and its legacy of resistance are invaluable in the successful negotiation of psychological space within an unfriendly physical place. The paradigm for negotiation of psychological space that is articulated in *Praisesong*—remoteness must be retained between the mind and the heart, as illus-trated by the Ibos's return walk to the motherland—must be instilled before the sinuous seduction by materialism occurs.

In Avey's tenth summer, when she and her aunt have walked to the Landing and the Ibo story has been retold, the child's impertinent ques-tion evokes the antithesis between what is written and what is spoken.[7] When Aunt Cuney says that the Ibos stepped across the water, a young Avey inquires why they didn't drown. The aunt holds the immediately repentant child in her fixed stare before she asks Avey whether her

New York Sunday-school books say Jesus drowned when he walked on water. The child's question implies an inherent danger of eyewitness accounts and oral narrative, both ways of shaping community for developing children. The written text of the dominant culture, valued above oral witness, traditionally has excluded or distorted the experiences of descendants of Africa. Western texts cannot be considered the most accurate means of shaping strategies of survival through meaningful community. The remnants of West African culture that survive in rurally isolated Tatem and connect it to the Caribbean island of Carriacou (where the rituals of ancestor worship and the Big Drum fete survive) are cultural stabilizers that are most effectively passed on through behavior, speech, and memory. Oral narrative, drawing on generations of fragments, becomes crucial in communicating the experience of connected communities, the places that Jean Toomer refers to in "Carma," where a goat path leads back to Africa (12).

Cultural indicators of a West African experience are purged from communities such as North White Plains, New York, the community of Avatara's wealthy widowhood. Even its name encodes racial sterility and ethnic exclusion. Away from emotional and physical proximity with nurturing qualities in Tatem, she resides in a community that silently demands her cultural self-effacement, a demand with which she begins complying even before her relocation there. In North White Plains, spiritual survival must be negotiated within the physical place and can only happen if one brings and closely guards distinct cultural properties.

According to Susan Willis, Marshall prefers the rural setting to the urban one because she "focuses on a segment of the American black population which, by access to the professions, has arrived at the wasteland of the suburbs. The city is thus equated with the breakdown of culture and not seen as the site for cultural renewal" (57). In the dream where Aunt Cuney forcibly tries to return Avey to the Landing, back to her rightful community, Avey imagines her neighbors' curiosity at the spectacle she and Aunt Cuney are creating, imagining that through no fault of her own she is fulfilling their stereotypical expectations. Avey's negligence in retaining her psychological space has eroded her psychic well-being. Therefore, she loses her self and connection to community after she becomes an adult, although such loss is not inevitable. Psychological space can be self-constructed in nonconducive physical space, but protection is essential. For several years, Jay and Avey, for example, successfully define their invulnerable space in their apartment on Halsey Street, which embodies the worst of what urban cities and capitalism inflict on the African-American psyche. Through cultural manifestations such as poetry, jazz, and dance, the couple retains psychological isolation and psychic health until the pressures of poverty and work overwhelm their space. Their example suggests an insidious infiltration of psychological space and the difficulty of its preservation, particularly in urban sites.

As early as *Brown Girl*, Marshall indicates her interest in the relationship between individual and place and the necessity of negotiating among various configurations of community. In the opening pages of *Brown Girl* she orchestrates the reader from the exterior Brooklyn street into an interior where tea is no longer served in the afternoons and where the quiet of the rooms clashes with the speech of the islanders, where the "parlor [is] full of ponderous furniture and potted ferns which the whites had left. . . . It was the museum of all the lives that had ever lived here" (5). And those former inhabitants had not been people of African descent. Selina stands poised at the top of the stairs in the pretentious world of a ten-year-old, momentarily pretending that she is one of them, that "they crowded around, fusing with her, [and she is] invested with their beauty and gentility" (5). It is a short-lived delusion, but it signals her attraction to and flexibility in negotiating among various communities, including the one of the dominant culture beyond the boundaries of Fulton Street. The stark whiteness of the Boyces' kitchen, often interpreted as emblematic of Silla's coldness, might more effectively be viewed as an indication of the family's basic incompatibility with the house and the city outside it. The "antiseptic white furniture and enameled white walls [of the] room seemed a strange unfeeling world which continually challenged [Deighton] to deal with it, to impose himself somehow on its whiteness" as he and Silla would have to do in the external world (22).

Brown Girl addresses communities in their broad and narrow circumference. The world outside the brownstone residence, though dominated by the communities of the majority culture, also offers the community of southern blacks, which the Barbadians reject. It is a curious though human phenomenon that, although their common origins, shared oppression, and exclusion on the basis of race, class, and gender join southern blacks and Afro-Caribbeans as a community, the Barbadians accept certain stereotypical views of black southerners, who in turn reciprocate. Both groups thus deny their shared historical origin. Geta Leseur acknowledges the Barbadian community as a vital force in the novel, calling it "powerful in its cohesion and demanding in its criteria for acceptance." She believes it "exudes wholeness, and in that wholeness strength" (119).

The Barbadian community emphasizes united negotiation through the majority community. The money that will be earned there, which in large measure validates immigration, will propel the Barbadians beyond their rented brownstone on Chauncey Street and farther than Fulton Street, a street of commerce that swirls and eddies with "a welter of dark faces" (37). Many of the immigrants succeed in the workplaces of the majority culture, but fracturing is the consequence. Silla and Deighton Boyce, though significant examples, are balanced by others. Deighton's mangled body and spirit symbolize his rejection not only by the workplace but also by his Barbadian community. (Deighton Boyce is discussed more fully in the section on race, class, and gender in chapter 3.) In his dejected, vulnerable state, he allows himself to be absorbed into another community, the cultlike religious followers of "Father," where his benumbed fractured self can be submerged and mostly forgotten in the frenzy of glorifying Father.

Writing about what she terms "the property of being" in *Brown Girl*, Vanessa D. Dickerson provocatively asserts that the "wall-less and thus roomless Kingdom Hall bespeaks no individuality but a mindless reduction of humanity into mass, not community" (7). Indeed, individuality is lost in the religious conglomerate, but the group satisfies the requirements for community. If Deighton is emblematic, all the members are in flight patterns of escape and benumbment. Many of them, like him, reel from psychological bruises received in hostile communities. Thus, their shared oppressions and rejections have brought them to Father's community. This group comprises a negative psychological community, not because of its religiosity but because it offers no structures designed to force the healing of a fractured self. Father's community is devoid of cultural myths, rituals, or other manifestations that might rescue Deighton from his drifting, ravaged state. The fractured self has merely moved to a different, less stressful arena.

Thus, two specific interest communities—the religious organization and the Barbadian Homeowners Association—are juxtaposed in *Brown Girl*. The former serves as a magnet for fractured and brutalized psyches; the latter is a player in the notions of capitalism. Both communities define themselves more through a psychocultural agenda than through demarcations of physical space. The Barbadian Homeowners Association nevertheless encourages negotiation, particularly in its quality of adaptation. Dickerson's claim that the brownstones "eventually move the mother forward *into community, into the Barbadian Association* and into schooling for herself as a practical nurse" (5, emphasis added) directly acknowledges the association as an active community. The coherency of the group around identified goals held by the dominant community—goals that would assimilate the Barbadians through economic avenues—illustrates an adaptive quality of negotiation in the strategy of survival. The association becomes a mediative group intended to assist the Barbadians in their transformation from recent immigrants—with customs and speech intact—to property owners. They will educate their young people with American values and accelerate their union with the dominant economics.

Suggie Skeete, a minor character, and Selina, the protagonist, illustrate significant variations in negotiating community. Suggie's example confirms the necessity for cultivating psychological space within the community of one's cultural kin if one operates contrary to the status quo. "When people see me coming they gon know it's [me]. Be Jees I ain gon be like them, all cut out of the same piece of cloth" (81). In refusing to labor exclusively for property ownership, she announces her differing philosophy. Her psychological space is her rented room in Silla's brownstone, where Suggie entertains the men whose physical love helps her survive in those other communities that disagree with her spirit, where the "snot-nose brats insult [her]." In the space that she salvages within Silla's house, Suggie prepares and eats native Caribbean foods and recalls her memories of island "spreeing" (80). She sustains herself through memories and sexual pleasure in a parochial community that eventually ejects her through Silla's agency, as it does Deighton, because neither of them conforms to its ideology. In its failure to serve both Suggie and Deighton, the community reveals the misdirection of its fractured membership. Although the group is bound by shared origin, oppression, and goals, it fails fully to serve itself.

Selina's coming-of-age process, in part, is her learning to negotiate among various communities and to claim membership in those that nurture her. Like Suggie, Selina's membership in the Barbadian community in New York City is her birthright. Her initiation into the community of adult Barbadian women, however, is attended by a small ceremony—an informal laying-on of hands when Silla's friend touches the young girl on her maturing breast. Selina literally rejects the touch and symbolically rejects the community of women. Nevertheless, the touch is a nurturing action that metaphorically signals Selina's membership among women. Selina's rejection, due to her immaturity, reverses to acceptance following an example of marginalization in the dominant community.

The fracturing that occurs when Selina is callously and directly touched by Euro-American racism takes place in an alien community. She has successfully danced her first solo in a white dance troupe. Intoxicated by the applause and praise of the audience and her dance group, Selina accepts an after-performance invitation, along with the other dancers. The new setting is another community "whose grandeur had been eclipsed by a modern apartment house that was all lightness and glass" (283). The girls' playful dancing and circle on the floor suggest their unity in the aftermath of Selina's success.

The exuberance of the evening can perhaps be blamed for her innocent expectations when she is summoned apart from the other girls for a chat with the hostess's mother. Praising her performance is not the purpose of the summons; reminding Selina of her community is the objective. After polite talk about herself, the dancer's mother begins questioning. "It was all like an inquisition somehow, where [Selina] was the accused, imprisoned in the wing chair, under the glaring lamp" (287). The mother's questions, followed by her tedious narrative about her West Indian housekeeper, tie Selina to the chair. She becomes terrified that somehow these people "sought to rob her of her substance and her self." What sends her reeling through the dark streets until she is breathless is her response to her own query, "What had brought her to this place?" Her answer, that it was "the part of her which had long hated her for her blackness" introduces the issue of self-hate, a constant characteristic of fracturing. Under the mother's pitiless racist barrage, Selina acknowledges her heretofore hidden disgust for her color. This event becomes "the one vivid memory of the evening . . . whenever she remembered it—all down the long years to her death" (289, 285).

Selina's first encounter with racist behavior is particularly painful because the event occurs where she thought she was among friends, because the woman's manner of insult reflects back to her Bajan community, and because it forces Selina to confront her own fears about her blackness. The evening would have been more devastating had she lacked the reassurance of psychological spaces within her own community. In part, the racial affront conjoins her with the community of Barbadian women more than Florie Trotman's touch on the breast. This membership is absolutely essential in psychically debilitating confrontations that occur in external communities where harsh forms of initiation often take place.

By emphasizing the young New York visitor to the Caribbean in "To Da-Duh, in Memoriam," Avatara's visits to Tatem in *Praisesong*, and Selina's initial youthfulness in *Brown Girl*, Marshall suggests that conscious introduction to multiple communities and to the necessity of negotiation is one of the significant rites of childhood. This knowledge is needed to survive the inevitable assaults upon the psyche that occur in the communities of the dominant culture.

History, Community, and Ritual in *The Chosen Place,*
The Timeless People

> [History] is a nightmare, as that Irishman said, and we haven't
>
> awakened from it yet. —*The Chosen Place*

Bourne Island and its villages, the setting of *The Chosen Place,* comprise Marshall's most intricate, elaborate, and extensively detailed physical setting. The opening pages of the novel describe an aerial view of the island—emphasizing its topography—from the perspective of arriving visitors. This view is followed by a car tour during which the description emphasizes the main town of New Bristol, the village of Spiretown, the community of Bournehills, and hills and ridges. This emphasis elevates and centers setting, particularly Bournehills, to pronounced visibility. In addition to setting, the history of Bournehills, with Cuffee Ned at the vortex, animates the initial introduction.

It becomes clear early in this work that the emphasis given to setting will extend equally to character. The novel depicts individuals who populate the community at its peasant level, those most bereft of any economic advancement: Gwen, who has a large family and works in the cane, carrying a heavy pile of it atop her head; Stinger, her husband, a cane worker; Vere, a young black man, who, not wanting to remain in Bournehills to burn his youth in the cane fields, burned it instead in the cane fields of Florida on a government-sponsored work scheme; Leesy, Vere's antique aunt, for whom time stopped when her husband was crushed beneath the cane rollers at the factory; Delbert, the proprietor of a local store and rum shop; the nameless children who visit Harriet, who have no carefree childhood but instead babysit their sisters and brothers; and Merle Kinbona, who epitomizes the paradoxes and incongruities of the community.

Marshall intermingles the communities and histories of other peoples with the isolated Caribbean island, primarily through the Jewish character, Saul Amron. Juxtaposing Saul and his Jewish heritage alongside the islanders conjoins, to some degree, their membership in metaphorically connected communities. Marshall effects another kind of convergence of world communities and their impact on each other through exploitative economic links that were forged long ago. These communities intersect in Bournehills through a manipulative London patron of Merle Kinbona and through Harriet Amron, the wealthy descendant of a northeastern U.S. community. This novel, more than any other, explores the perspective of community as a timeless entity greater than its population and as an entity of paradox, both mutable and immutable.

Harriet Amron and the absentee controllers of the sugar industry represent specific kinds of communities in interaction with the island. In this novel in particular, Marshall offers a discourse on relationships between communities and their institutions. Bournehills, as an example of a Caribbean island, becomes the convergence point, just as the Caribbean became a pivotal point in the triangle trade. Industry on the island is largely controlled by absentee owners and managers and comprises the most effective symbol of European neocolonial dominance of the Caribbean. The power of the European community is kept palpably present, for example, when Cane Vale, the only sugar-processing plant, is arbitrarily closed after the estate crops are processed but before the small crops of the Bournehills farmers are harvested.

Like the European community, Harriet Amron recalls an ancestral history of profitable involvement in the triangle trade and the weight of power and privilege that has accrued from it. More specifically, one of her female ancestors had invested in and profited from human and nonhuman cargo. The United Corporation of America, or Unicor, represents a merger of family businesses in Philadelphia, including Harriet's ancestor. The commercial group has created a research institute, which then creates a center that is funding Saul's project in the islands. Expansion over the years has connected Unicor with Kingsley and Sons, the British sugar-industry giant in the islands. These business links are "like some elaborate rail or root system, [that] endlessly crosses the world, binding it up" (37). The paradox of the center's involvement in Bournehills is easily transparent; it is funding an anthropological and philanthropical expert to hypothesize the solution to a problem that, in significant part, its parent organization has created.

Critical discussions of *The Chosen Place* have minimally involved Harriet Amron, but she has a vital symbolic role if any reconciliation of communities is to be possible.[8] In such a lengthy and tedious process, for communities and individuals alike, the initial requirements include casting aside hegemonic proclivities, transcending false barriers and misperceptions about cultural and racial differences, and admitting responsibility for past injuries. Because the West perpetuates its arrogance and only pays lip service to reconciliation—through economic development schemes like that of the center or through the tourist industry that benefits its creators more than the islanders—Harriet, as the West's symbol, enters the island well prepared to resist its mystical ability to compel confrontation with the past. Because she inures herself to the past and especially to the role that her ancestors played (about which she knows) in generating the psychic fracturing of Africans displaced to the Caribbean, she cannot survive. Her solid resistance to the mystical spell that Bournehills works, which motivates Saul and Merle to confront their pasts and enables their psychic health, seals her doom. Harriet consistently excludes from conscious consideration the eccentricies of Merle, who epitomizes the psychological displacement of the islanders, the ravages of Westernization on both individual and land, and "[embodies] West Indian history" (Rahming 131). In so doing, Harriet effectively closes herself to meaningful island intimacy in spite of her superficial connections with the women and children.

Nowhere is Harriet's cultural arrogance and hegemonic impulse more telling than during the carnival parade; infused by Cuffee Ned's spirit of resistance, the revelers refuse to heed her efforts to redirect their passage. Blatantly ignoring her presence amounts to a reversal of the powerful/powerless binary. Harriet is not only powerless but arbitrarily expelled from their presence by their collective force: "She swatted away at them the way one would at a swarm of flies, and they, as indifferent to her blows as they had been to her insistent voice before, continued to sing and fire the guns and perform the reckless plunging dance. . . . But in the next moment they were surging forward again in a furious melee that saw her thrown from their midst against the warehouse door" (296).

This experience of impotence is repeated in three other stunning rejections concerning issues of dominance and capitulation. Merle savagely dismisses Harriet's offer to finance Merle's departure from the island to separate her and Saul; Saul refuses Harriet's manipulation of his career through her directive to the center that the Bournehills project be terminated; and Saul dissolves his relationship to Harriet. Her response to impotence is self-destruction. It seems a predictably fitting conclusion, though an unfortunate one.

Conversely, Saul, because of his legacy of oppression as a Jew and because his anthropological research has situated him in victimized settings, cares for humans and respects their community. Although he is susceptible to introspection about his personal life, he is unhampered by the desire to command and control. Harriet is out of time in the Bournehills community because her concept of time, Western and linear, prohibits recovery of the past. The concept of time that informs Bournehills—cyclical time—allows recovery and offers a "constant source of new beginnings, of ontological renewal" (Ray, 41). This view of time explains the animated immediacy of Cuffee in the conscience of Bournehills and the people's timeless quality.[9] It also addresses, in part, Harriet's resistance to the spirit of the street marchers at carnival.

Bournehills as setting operates both literally and metaphorically. At the metaphorical level, as focal community it epitomizes other demographic regions whose natural resources have been subordinated to economic advancement—"the Peruvian Andes, the highlands of Guatemala. Chile. Bolivia, where [Saul] had once worked briefly among the tin miners. Honduras . . . Southern Mexico. And the spent cotton lands of the Southern United States. . . . Every place that had been wantonly used" (*The Chosen Place*, 100).

On the literal level, physical place and human community are unified and inexchangeable. What happens to the natural resources exerts a proportional impact on the psyche of the population. The population of Bournehills, mostly sugarcane workers, reflects the ravaged land in their physiques, a feature that adds to their mystique. Although the action of the novel encompasses the entire island, Bournehills stands out as a Third World community resistant to modernization. Although their resistance becomes a joke among black islanders of other communities—"One almost begins to suspect that [Bournehills] chooses not to [change], for some perverse reason. . . . There's no understanding those people" (62, 58)—their opposition to forced modernity is their refusal to allow others to make decisions concerning their lives. They protect their intimacies and complexities from probing visitors even as Saul seeks intimacy with the land and its people to institute responsible changes.

Layers of intricate structure complicate Marshall's story of a research team's entry into the community as the preface to an improvement project and of Merle Kinbona's self-regathering. Aside from the delineation of topography, Marshall's representation of the island's various classes as a product of history and of a community patterned by myth and ritual signals the comprehensive stratification of this novel. Dorothy Dennison convincingly contends that Marshall, in constructing the work to reflect the traditional African view of time, organizes the book to simulate the major divisions of the African agricultural year (230).

Similarly, Hortense Spillers offers "four circles of involvement—myth, history, ritual, and ontology—[that] identify the primary structural and dramatic features of the work" ("Chosen Place, Timeless People," 152). Marshall's concepts of interdependence and of continuity indicate her balancing of community and individual along historical infinitude.

Her attentiveness to history and to a disrupted community is evident in the epigraph that frames the narrative, borrowed from the Tiv of West Africa: "Once a great wrong has been done, it never dies. People speak the words of peace, but their hearts do not forgive. Generations perform ceremonies of reconciliation but there is no end." The evocation of slavery in the epigraph becomes more specific in the physical juxtaposition of Bourne Island with the continent of Africa. The island "fac[es] east, the open sea, and across the sea, hidden beyond the horizon, the colossus of Africa" (13). The Atlantic on one side of Bournehills, in fact, seems continuously to mourn the Africans who died during the Middle Passage: "With a sound like that of the combined voices of the drowned raised in a loud unceasing lament—all those nine million and more it is said, who in their enforced exile, their Diaspora, had gone down between this point and the homeland lying out of sight to the east" (106). This connectedness becomes a subtext that animates the narrative, for the diasporic link repeatedly surfaces through the emphasis on historical antecedents, the immutability of Bournehills, and Cuffee Ned's resistance to oppression. Harriet Amron's presence and ancestral background establish the obverse side of the triangular relationship among these communities. The novel thus evokes Africa, the United States, and the Caribbean as contiguous entities that, once bound through a commercialism that included human beings, may not easily divorce their affiliations.

The past competes with the present in Bournehills. The structure of power, represented by the monied British industrialists or the landowners, and the consistently poor, epitomized by those who work in sugarcane fields, remains as wide as it was during slavery in spite of the emergence of a black professional class. The class structure of the island, which mirrors its history, is reflected in the population at Sugars, a popular nightclub, where the patrons are "all shades and colors, castes and classes." The nightclub, housed on the second floor of a building that was formerly a barracoon, underscores not only the haunting presence of the past but also the distinctiveness of class and the necessity of psychological space on the island (79). The "solid, moneyed men . . . all of them white, some foreigners, but mostly . . . Bourne Island whites" occupy the choicest seats in the club, just as they occupy the choicest places in the community structure (87). Enlivened by rum and music, the dancing patrons "appeared caught up in violent combat, with the room, divided as it were between great areas of shadow and light, serving as an arena the size of the world" (92). Dance becomes a metaphor for survival and a mask for subduing the chaos that seems ever threatening.

Like Marshall, some other African-American women feature history prominently in their fiction. In Gayl Jones's *Corregidora*, the maternal ancestors of the protagonist, Ursa Corregidora, demand that generations of female children be told of the abuses and of the Brazilian slavemaster, Corregidora. Because official documentation of slavery is scant or has been destroyed and because its most outrageous violations were probably never recorded, oral transmission becomes the only means of fixing the experience in the memory of new generations. This emphasis on history and its role in the consciousness of future generations occurs in various configurations.[10] Marshall's configuration, like Jones's, requires oral transmission but relies on carnival pageantry. Perhaps more significantly, Marshall merges the individual with history and its reflection in community. For Bournehills people, their most inspiriting history is vested in the cultural hero Cuffee Ned, who, with his cohorts, struck a resounding blow against slavery on the island and temporarily freed his community. Their reverence to his memory, in fact, mediates between the text of history and the glory of myth.[11]

History, ritual, myth, and festival pattern and structure the Bournehills community. The memory of Cuffee Ned's successful resistance and his leadership unifies and animates the people amidst the poverty, deprivation, and soul-killing hard labor of the cane fields. This positive use of history removes it from stagnant reverence of the past and elevates it to prominence in the daily existence of the community. Bournehills' use of history amounts to a rejection of its concept in the West as a chronological record, the domain of academicians and students, who learn it by rote in school. History in Bournehills reflects Allan Nevins's view of history as enabling communities "to grasp their relationship with the past, and to chart on general lines their immediate forward course" (quoted in Hamerow, 209). Cuffee Ned's resistance lingers tangibly to shape the people's responses to the present. Their landscape embodies his opposition in the prominence of Pyre Hill, where he burned the manor of his enslaver. The community offers Cuffee Ned to its visitors as the best part of the legacy as survivors of slavery. Merle Kinbona tells the story of Cuffee Ned's torching of Pyre Hill to the newly arrived research team—Saul, his wife, Harriet, and his statistician associate, Allen Fusco—during their first few hours on the island. As Saul journeys in Bournehills to meet the community, he finds a gathering of men in the local store, two of whom are engaged in heated debate about the details of Cuffee's takeover of the estate. Theirs is not an isolated evening but a recurrent and stylized diatribe.

The revolt occurred on Pyre Hill, site of Percy Bryam's mansion.

Surprising Percy Bryam at night, Cuffee captured him, burned his estate house, and later that night yoked him to the mill wheel (as he had once yoked workers), where he died. Under Cuffee Ned's leadership, the slaves resisted government forces, sealed off the ridge, and for two years defended themselves and lived independently. British troops finally overpowered them and ended the siege. The fire on Pyre Hill burned "for five long years, the books say—long after Cuffee Ned was dead and the revolt put down, the old hill continued to burn" (102).

The story of Cuffee's revolt, affirmed by written, official accounts (what the books say), is balanced by its transformation into the regions of myth. The revolt has historical precedent in the numerous uprisings that occurred in the Caribbean islands, the most famous being Toussaint L'Ouverture's rebellion in Haiti. But the story of Cuffee Ned most probably reflects revolts in Barbados led by a slave also named Cuffee. This attention to history, to an actual event rather than to an elaborate folk story, is significant given the mythic dimensions that Marshall attaches to Cuffee's presence.[12] Through the conversion of history into myth the event becomes the community's attempt at sociocultural assertion and self-empowerment. The mythic conversion supersedes history as it exists in books. As a student of history in London, Merle knows the official text of the Caribbean past, which is disallowed in the schools. She was a history teacher, but when she refused to stop telling the story of Cuffee Ned, she was fired: "The headmaster wanted her to teach the history that was down in the books, that told all about the English." She refused because that history "made it look like black people never fought back. Well, they fired her in no time flat" (32). (Merle Kinbona's role in the novel and her psychic reintegration are discussed in chapter 3.)

Thus, official accounts of history are inadequate if they skew the events of the past through distortion or omission. Myth, however, may infuse an event with vitality, and when the method of communication is oral transmission, the event fosters inclusion. Ferguson, for example, becomes one with the narrative of Cuffee in the shop: "And as he talked he danced, a taut, graceful, highly stylized dance full of little menacing leaps and feints. . . . He was shouting as he lunged forward. . . . I say Cuffee held off the whole damn British regiment for upward of six months. Not a jack-man of them could get pas' Cleaver's High Wall all that time." Stinger replied, "Fergy, I don't give a fuckarse what you say. . . . It wasn't no six months. How could he have held out against a whole regiment that long? It was only two, three months at the most, I tell you" (122).

Ironically, even during this conversion of history into myth, Ferguson refers to the historical account, legitimated by its printed form: "I'm the one after all who went down to the library in town and read the big book there that tells all about him" (122). To Saul's ears, the men "had imposed their own stinging rhythms and harsh, atonal accent upon the language, had infused it with a raw poetry, transforming it, making it their own" (122). Through this process, official history, distanced from the community in language and tone, returns to them by their own initiative. The Bournehills community has transformed history to myth, not only making it accessible and usable but also converting it into a participatory enterprise.

The accessibility is evident in Cuffee's appropriation as a symbol of ideal community and as a cultural hero whose resistance and success crystallize a concept worthy of reattainment and reenactment. "Cuffee had us planting the fields together, I tell you," Ferguson cried. "Reaping our crops together, sharing whatsomever we had with each other. We was a people then, man; and it was beautiful to see!" (139). Writing about Marshall's use of myth in Cuffee, Jacqueline de Weever accurately assesses him as revitalizing "the myth of the hero become dying god, whose story becomes a life-giving ritual for his people. . . . Identification with the various parts of the myth is necessary for the myth to work its healing powers on the community, and the villagers, both participants and audience, immerse themselves totally in the story" (41, 43).

Weever's statement includes the men in the shop as well as the island spectators during carnival. The Bournehills community re-creates the revolt as the annual masque for carnival, a practice that earns them the opprobrium of the spectators even as the tense action compels the spectators' visceral participation. Thus, history revitalizes and cleanses the present. The marchers recontextualize Cuffee Ned's revolt, exhuming the ancestral blow against oppression and rejoicing in its unity. They use it to infuse their own resistance against the imposition of Western modeling on their economy and lives.

Carnival is structurally significant both as the title of book 3 of *The Chosen Place* and as a community event. In fact, one indication of the thoroughness with which community is conceptualized is the incorporation of holidays and religious days that traditionally have served as a means for ritual realization.[13] Carnival is among several festive days that help define the sociocultural traditions of Bournehills. The community year, divided by when it is "in crop" and "out of crop" time is punctuated by carnival, the first holiday of the year, almost at its center, "two days—Monday and Tuesday preceding Ash Wednesday" (268). Victor Turner points out that carnival, as a feature of the cosmological calendar, is differentiated from ordinary historical time: "Truly carnival is the denizen of a place that is no place, and a time that is no time, even where that place is a city's main plaza, and that time can be found on an ecclesiastical calendar" (76). According to Roger Abrahams, anthropological research has shown that, especially in noncosmopolitan societies, " 'the work of the gods' conjoins fun and seriousness, juxtaposing them as one means of attaining community. . . . Play is carried out in defiance as well as for renewal" ("An American Vocabulary," 177). Writing about carnival in *The Chosen Place,* Simon Gikandi says that it "obscures as well as discloses: they suspend time and mask the drudgery of everyday life. . . . For outside observers, the carnivalesque is obscure; for the peasants of Bourneville [*sic*], it discloses a collective genealogy and perpetuates their 'national spirit' " (187). Their national spirit is inseparable from Cuffee Ned's elimination of plantocrat Percy Bryam. Their solemn reenactment of Cuffee's revolt, though it disrupts an otherwise jovial and spirited day, has its justification.

Myth becomes ritualized in the reenactment of the Cuffee Ned revolt. Max Gluckman has emphasized the importance of rituals of rebellion. People act out roles normally denied them, he says, and the ceremonies are one example of ritual inversion, by which he means a psychological catharsis. Rituals are symbolic and transformational (quoted in Crocker, 59). During carnival, then, the Bournehills population, assuming the righteous position of rebellion, ejects the oppressors and replaces them with jubilant, victorious freedom. Communal divisiveness is replaced by unity. Bournehills peasants, the immutable underclass, take charge of the future in viewing Cuffee Ned's spirit as the ideal symbol of community through which they might renew themselves.

Margaret Mead identifies another capability of ritual that is apparent in the masque performance: to recreate an intense past emotional experience (91), a process that obviously occurs in the performers and the spectators along the route. The march behind the Pyre Hill float, prior to the enacting of the revolt, conjures up the doom of past enforced marches, "of legions marching bound together over a vast tract, iron fitted into dank stone wall, chains—like those to an anchor—rattling in the deep holds of ships, and exile in an unknown inhospitable land— an exile bitter and irreversible in which all memory of the former life and of the self as it had once been had been destroyed. . . . *The bones that served as the props to their spirit might have been broken*" (emphasis added; 282).

The effectiveness of the performance can be gauged by the blurring between reality and performance for some spectators. One young boy really believes that he is warning Percy Bryam, and an elderly man later attacks Ferguson as Bryam. The marchers resurrect their rebellious ancestors resisting the British regiment, and upon victory, the band plays a "hymn of jubilation and victory" (285). Those who had reenacted marching slaves dance in triumphant celebration of Cuffee Ned's indomitable spirit, but they also conclude his story, telling how, like the maroons of Jamaica and Negroes of Guiana, the rebels lived independently until the British ruthlessly crushed them and killed Cuffee. They repeat the masque the entire afternoon but cease to repeat the revolutionaries' defeat; instead, they end with Cuffee's victory. Although the parade observers initially disparage this annual repetition of the Bournehills masque, they are compelled to experience its meaning in spite of themselves. Thus, the ritual, at least temporarily, enjoins the

community across class, race, and gender lines. The stylized march, performance components, repetition, symbolic value, and transformational
element mark this enactment of myth as ritual.

Several far-reaching consequences of carnival mark its significance as
both event and narrative-structuring device. Saul and Merle, in losing
the barriers that had prevented verbal intimacy, achieve physical intimacy. Vere, having disgorged his preoccupation with the mother of his
dead child, reembraces love with a new woman in the post-carnival
atmosphere. Allen confronts his homosexuality. Only Harriet, of the
major characters, denies that she is fundamentally altered by her impotence among the carnival marchers. For a suspended moment in time,
the sons and daughters of peasants become progenitors of power. The
solidarity is powerful because it derives from a common sense of purpose and it is self-fulfilling and self-enabling—not directed against
anyone. On the literal level, Harriet merely becomes an inadvertent
victim and undesirable presence. Her ethnocentric tradition and community, having left her unprepared to cope with such thorough dis-
missal, have also undermined her psychic survival ability. Spillers notes
the significance of waterways in *The Chosen Place*, with the Atlantic
and Caribbean Sea converging off the island ("Chosen Place," 155). It
is appropriate that Harriet drown at the juncture of those two bodies
of water, merging both the literal and metaphorical resonance of her
character with the thematic convergence of communities.

Carnival and the Cuffee Ned performance are preceded by another
ritual—a Sunday-morning hog killing—that fits expediently into the
narrative as the last chapter of part 2. This juxtaposition of a weekly
community ritual with an annual island ritual emphasizes a regular
event that functions as a psychocultural enterprise on a smaller scale
than carnival, but with similar benefits. Just as carnival, generally, the
Cuffee Ned masque specifically, and even the rum shop gatherings are
rituals of spiritual renewal, the hog killing reinforces male camaraderie and community and provides a safe forum for venting repression.
As a scheduled activity, the Sunday hog killing punctuates and stabilizes the onset of another cycle of toil. It corresponds to Christopher
Crocker's observation that societies meet situations of crisis with ritual,

thereby demonstrating the enduring validity of certain principles of order. Ritual, he continues, concerns humans' relationships to other people and to institutions, spirits, and nature (48). The underclass of Bournehills men and women, most of its population, lives in a perpetual crisis of existence. Symbolically, they massacre the invisible forces that daily murder their spirit and sap their physical strength as the pig is killed. The assembled men all participate in its demise.

The religious images that Marshall interjects in the description of the hog killing makes the sacrifice motif unavoidable. Profane and sacred and religious and pagan are juxtaposed during this ritual of animal sacrifice, where the atmosphere is overtly charged because this particular hog killing precedes carnival. Thus, it seems that the weekly value of this event is subordinated to its different purpose as a sacrifice that might insure a successful carnival. The hog is special, Leesy's "great white sow" that has been preserved for a special occasion. The imagery and the way in which the men handle the hog also confirm that this event is more ritual than routine. The men make a fire in the half-dark, predawn light, ready a receptacle to receive the carcass and the animal's blood, and erect a scaffold that has "been raised like a cross" (252). In a discussion of ritual and animal sacrifice, Ray's observations about the significance of the preparatory and concluding phases of sacrifice seem present in the hog killing. The specifics of sacralizing "the time, place, and victims of the sacrifice and all those who participate in it" might not be achieved in this hog killing, but the time, place, type of animal, and manner of death are predetermined (252). In African tradition, the animal victim is a mediating symbol of both worlds because it resides in the human world but also belongs to the spiritual realm.

The men give human characteristics to the pig, thus anchoring it to both worlds, as when one of them tells it not to follow him for he cannot save it (253). It has been "crying," they say, probably calling "My god, my god, why hast thou foresaken me?" (253). The pig's death occurs "at the moment the new day [is] being born" and is connected with the symbolism of Christian communion: The moon was "wafer thin now, a substanceless eucharistic host" (257). The depilation of the pig becomes a communal act—all the men participate. According to Ray, this

act satisfies another need of ritual—its desacralization so that participants safely return to the normal human world. The desacralization is
achieved through a mood change in the men. Where they had been almost reverent, they become "brusque, impersonal, cold, even cruel" as
they tear off the hair, "methodically pummeling the sow's inert carcass"
(257). Once the tail has been removed and placed in the fire to cook, the
men hang the carcass on the scaffold so that it can be gutted. They then
pass around a bottle of rum and each man bites from the roasted tail.
This sharing of flesh, according to Ray, solidifies the "spiritual bond
between worshipers and the god or spirits to whom a portion is also
given." This sacrifice thus conforms to the basic threefold structure
that Ray identifies: consecration, invocation-immolation, communion-
purification. Socially, it has affirmed male camaraderie and reinforced
them as a group (79).[14] It is significant that Saul participates in this rite,
including eating the half-cooked pork, because his activity joins him in
sincerity with the male islanders whose community he wishes to help.

The annual ritual of carnival and the weekly one of hog killing
enhance Marshall's attentiveness to the requirements of community
as social structure. Her synthesis of the interactions of community,
history, and ritual in Bourne Island life illustrates the effect of these
entities and Marshall's skill in integrating them so thoroughly in *The
Chosen Place*.

Legacies of Community and History in *Daughters*

There is a Third World in every First World, and vice versa.

—Trinh T. Minh-ha

Ursa McKenzie, a transplanted West Indian from Marshall's fictional
island of Triunion, stands on an overpass and looks below to see a new
superhighway bisecting the black community of Midland City, New
Jersey: "Triunion! Triunion! all over again! While she was still in high
school, the P and D Board had completely rebuilt the road between the
airport and town, turning it into a highway for the benefit of the tourists

and the would-be money people, with a section that bypassed Armory Hill altogether, and that had cost a fortune. Where am I? Which place? What country? Is there no escaping that island? She stood for the longest time on the overpass above what had once been DeSalles and Marion streets, putting the questions to herself" (292).

Estelle, an African American transplanted to Triunion from Connecticut (and Ursa's mother) similarly superimposes Triunion communities on black urban areas in the United States: "I've really come to see things here and in the States in pretty much the same light. There's the same work to be done. I drive past Armory Hill, the big slum we have here, and I could be driving through all the Harlems in the States" (224).

Through the juxtaposition of these communities, Marshall foregrounds several significant issues in *Daughters*. For example, she aligns sociopolitical problems in the physical settings of predominantly black populations, settings assumed to be widely disparate because some are located in the United States and others exist in the Third World. Her juxtaposition highlights a perplexing phenomenon: social, political, and economic liabilities in so-called Third World countries exhibit visible similarities to those that plague blacks in First World countries. Textually, Marshall links these communities through the physical placement of Ursa and Estelle McKenzie and through referential codes that are enhanced by their mother-daughter relationship.[15] Marshall targets the vagaries of political decisions that dismiss the physical and psychological unity necessary to the black community. Although she tellingly juxtaposes Caribbean and U.S. urban communities, she emphasizes the communities of Triunion.

In a discussion of culture and criticism, W. J. T. Mitchell writes that "traditional cultural exports [have] tended to support the authority of the imperial center. . . . Critical movements such as feminism, Black Studies, and Western Marxism . . . are in the paradoxical position of bringing a rhetoric of decolonization from the imperial center. Perhaps this is why so many imaginative writers of the Third World . . . look with wary fascination on contemporary criticism, unsure whether it is a friendly collaborator in the process of decolonization" (16–17).

Ways of thinking about colonial hegemony and subjectification become less problematic when the marginalized control their own representation. Their perspective is automatically distanced from the discourse of the center. Claiming both African-American and Afro-Caribbean heritage, Marshall illustrates a psychocultural convergence with both groups by consistently incorporating their communities, characters, and politics in her work. Her discourse on the disablying remnants and propped-up structures of postcolonialism in Caribbean communities can only be read as a rhetoric of decolonization. Her fiction critically questions the fracturing of both communities and the consequent stress on the human psyche.

The political continuum between *The Chosen Place* and *Daughters* reflects Tejaswini Niranjana's observation that "the postcolonial subject, nation, context is therefore still scored through by an absentee colonialism. In economic and political terms, the former colony continues to be dependent on the ex-rulers or the 'West.' In the cultural sphere (using *cultural* to encompass not only art and literature but other practices of subjectification as well), in spite of widely employed nationalistic rhetoric, decolonization is slowest in making an impact" (8).

Postcolonialism in Marshall's Caribbean is most firmly entrenched in politics and economics. In *Daughters*, familial relationships, character location, and memory are the primary components through which the author explores a debilitating postcolonial mentality on the island of Triunion and reveals their curious reflection in U.S. cities. Primus Mackenzie, a British-educated Triunionite and aspiring politician, marries Estelle, a politically astute African-American woman from Connecticut, who relocates with him to the island. They raise their daughter, Ursa (the novel's protagonist), there but send her to her maternal grandparents in Connecticut for her high school and college education. As a young adult, Ursa lives in New York City, works in Midland City, New Jersey, and occasionally returns to Triunion, thus conjoining the U.S. and Triunion communities. She is young enough when she is sent to the States to embrace African-American culture alongside her Caribbean roots. In part, mediating Primus's influence was Estelle's objective for Ursa's relocation. Primus Mackenzie (called the PM, an acronym for his name and for prime minister, the political position that his community believes he will eventually hold) approaches the stature of a tragic figure flawed by complex contradictory impulses. When necessary, Estelle stabilizes Primus's impulses by refocusing the community in his political strategies.

The Mackenzie family forms a triad, a prime structuring device of the text. The Mackenzies' perspectives are enhanced by the creation of a similar triad in Triunion—Primus, Celestine (the family's maid), and Astral Forde (Primus's lover). In New York, still another triad—Ursa, Vincereta "Viney" Daniels (her girlfriend), and Lowell Carruthers (her lover)—elucidate increasingly distant relationships between individual and community. The novel depicts an intricate association of human relationships—husbands and wives, daughters and fathers, lovers, and friends; conversely, however, the novel also shows endangered connections between individual and community. In historically oppressed settings, *Daughters* insists on unflinching service to the community, an obligation secured by cultural legacies of opposition to oppression. Community salvation involves more than identifying problems and solving them, for the widening spiral of leftover oppression envelopes successive generations.

Primus, a newly elected, black, government official with a politically astute and energetic wife, initially believes that he can effect political and economic change and terminate the stasis of postcolonial subjectification. Yet outside forces overlay the various communities of Triunion, deterring efforts at economic autonomy and stability. Although home rule is in effect, the ruling government remains a puppet government. Nevertheless, the illusion that the translated subjects somehow are responsible for the poverty of their existence remains. This process of domination, neither linear nor uncomplicated, infiltrates whatever home rule the islanders claim and undermines their much-needed improvements.

Over the course of the more than thirty-four-year span of the novel, Primus paradoxically becomes a visible exponent of postcolonialism. The subjected are transformed in attitude, unconsciously acquiescing to power inequities. By the novel's end, Primus's entrapment is complete, and he has lost sight of his initial goals of bettering his community. Instead, he supports an investment scheme that will transform the best oceanfront property on the island into a tourist/business complex with its own airport and other Western amenities.

Part of Primus's complexity is that he seems to have been tainted by colonial precepts even as a political novice and a newlywed. As an inexperienced but spirited economic reformer, he displays separatist behavior, which, although barely perceptible, is a sign of class consciousness. His acquisitions preclude any intimacy of identification with ordinary islanders: his imported Buick, impractical for Triunion's tiny roads; his palatial home in the best part of town; even his imported middle-class, fair-skinned wife, whose color is very important in West Indian culture. Primus's social conscience makes him one of the community, but his Western education values the individual over the community and independence over interdependency. This antithesis reflects Frantz Fanon's philosophy about relationships between Europeans and colonized peoples: because "the principle of reciprocal exclusivity" affects all relations between the two groups, "the colonized man is an envious man" (39). Brainwashed by the oppressor's values, the subject, even with self-government, finds cultural independence obscured. In the case of a colonized intellectual like Primus, the situation is especially complicated.

Marshall lends symbolic import to Primus's contradictions through an incident involving the rape of a mare that young Primus witnesses (152) in the Mackenzies' yard. The rape may be correlated with the child's subsequent behavior and therefore read as emblematic of his compulsion to dominate, but it also can illustrate his adult behavior and relationship with his community. Primus's mother uses the event to inculcate in him a personal responsibility for his own social elevation. She emphasizes his subordinate class status relative to the near-white boys who will be his classmates and will come "from Garrison row and Raleigh Hill in town where the great people-them live! . . . And because they come from Garrison Row and Raleigh Hill and have those names and that color they're going to feel themselves better than you" (159). But even these threatening boys diminish in comparison to the whites from England, the United States, and Canada who own the businesses and banks. Her lessons in island class structure and her charges to Primus—to surpass them scholastically, to acquire the money and other possessions befitting an adult male, including a wife—are manifested in the adult father and husband, who indeed provides a home on Garrison Row for his wife and daughter.

Education in the town schools, however, is the "principle agency in the business of institutionalized violence," according to Bill Riviere (quoted in Cudjoe, 20). Similarly, Walter Rodney comments that "colonial schooling [is] education for subordination, exploitation, the creation of mental confusion and the development of underdevelopment" (quoted in Cudjoe, 20). Speaking particularly about Puerto Rico, Juan Angel Silen's observations reinforce those above but also underscore the psychic fracturing endemic to the educational experience: "As a ruling-class instrument it penalizes students and teachers to make them conform to an authoritarian structure. It aims to brutalize them by psychological manipulation" (quoted in Cudjoe, 21). These statements, to some degree, explain the contradictions of Primus's behavior as well as his compromised allegiance to the community.

The aftermath of a history of both slavery and European colonial hegemony embroils him, the other islanders, and his American wife. Primus's unreconciled contradictions, among other factors, restrict his usefulness to a community that he claims to love and serve; these inconsistencies engender unverbalized conflict between him and his daughter, Ursa. Although he overtly serves the community as an elected member of the House and, with Estelle's sensible direction, works during the early years of his marriage to effect change, there is little improvement. His proposals for economic relief are dismissed or ignored by the financial wizards from Britain, Canada, or the United States, who prefer to invest funds in tourism and its accoutrements—developed seaports, hotel chains, communication systems, and airports (239).

Primus's contradictions and the immutable island conditions torment Estelle's spirit, as is symbolized by her disinclination to nourish her body. She embodies communal consciousness, but her well-intentioned efforts are futile against the postcolonial mentality and infrastructure.

Estelle initially envisions her marriage to a Triunion political figure as a union of romance and politics (a reincarnated Congo Jane and Will Cudjoe, revered island revolutionaries), anticipating that Primus's party will gain power and begin transforming the economy. Her disillusionment after years of minimal advance is epitomized in the game of Statues at a public political reception, where she assumes the attitude of a stone figure immune to insult, disappointment, and rejection. Her 'statues' becomes a self-protective refuge for the psyche during a moment of unendurable political machination. Like the catatonic states of Merle Kinbona in *The Chosen Place*, Estelle's frozen attitude shuts down her yawp of disillusionment, which might have alienated the investor who insisted on tourist-related investments that would benefit Primus himself. As Marshall's fiction reaffirms, black communities may expect positive change when the masses advocate it; otherwise, anticipating equitable dispensation of resources from a government—even one that includes black elected officials—is courting disillusionment.

Although Estelle never articulates her perceptions about Primus's contradictions, her decision to educate Ursa in Connecticut suggests Estelle's vigilance concerning her daughter's values. Moreover, during Ursa's childhood in the 1960s, Estelle crops her daughter's hair into an Afro, thus demonstrating generational continuity in their relationship to community, including Estelle's brother, who took part in the Freedom Rides of the same era. Estelle also implants in Ursa the value of community and of Triunion's historical resistance, taking her to pay homage to the statues erected to honor Congo Jane and Will Cudjoe. This background positions Ursa solidly within the two communities, where she is passionate about both.

Ironically, the political and economic disappointments endemic to Third World black communities afflict those in the United States as well. Marshall's juxtaposition of Triunion's communities with one representative urban black community reveals disconcerting similarities. In Midland City, for example, a black mayor elected by a grass-roots constituency fails to propose legislation that will benefit blacks. Instead, an expressway will bisect the inner-city to provide smooth transportation for those living beyond its borders. Ursa's observation at the beginning of this chapter points to a similar decision in Triunion, where the highway provides comfort for tourists while roads remain almost impassable through black settlements. In both communities, poor housing, drugs, unemployment, and poor health care stifle and fracture people's lives.

The secondary status experienced by the black citizenry of Midland City and Triunion is countered in *Daughters* by a legacy of resistance to oppression. Gabriel Prosser, Harriet Tubman, and innumerable others in the United States have counterparts in the Caribbean. *Daughters* projects this legacy, primarily investing it in Congo Jane and Will Cudjoe but referencing other rebels as well. Their vision and sacrifice, commemorated by a monument, informs the conscience of Triunion's population and of the novel's protagonist. Congo Jane and Will Cudjoe, an enslaved couple, spurned bondage to become "coleaders, coconspirators, lovers, consorts, [and] friends" (336). Their relationship and their leadership embody effective resistance. Their monument reminds the descendants of Amerindians and Africans that their heritage is a continuum of defiance, that "resistance, not acquiescence, is the core of history" (Herbert Aptheker, quoted in Crane, 11). Visiting the monument assumes ritualistic qualities when Estelle takes young Ursa there to touch Congo Jane's toes. Ursa, in turn, brings her black American friend, Viney, so that she and her son might pay homage to the couple. They provide an impetus for Ursa's personal resistance when she chooses to privilege the communal over the personal.

During election rallies, the community's assembly at the monument may be interpreted as a desire to reinvigorate the spirit of resistance symbolized by the stone figures. This spirit, capable of spontaneous eruption, explains the government's decision to locate the monuments "all the way in the country, behind God's back, where scarcely anybody can get to see them, so as not to offend the white people in town . . . far back from the road, so that not even the few people passing by can see them" (375). Concealing the monument fails to deter an insurgent ardor for cultural reclamation, however. The resistance that is the legacy of descendants of Africans in the Caribbean, according to

Seldwyn Cudjoe, becomes "an aesthetic-political quality and structuring element" in the literature of the West Indies. Resistance becomes "ideological content" (65).

Will Cudjoe and Congo Jane are metaphorically situated at the center of the continuum of Western hegemony that links Triunion and its sister sites in the United States. Ursa's Euro-American adviser promptly rejects her proposal for her senior thesis project—to study the "relatively egalitarian and mutually supportive relationships that existed between the bondsmen and women and their significance for and contribution to the various forms of resistance to enslavement. . . . Her topic, the sources . . . her methodology, and most of all her thesis—which he found highly doubtful—all were unacceptable" (11). The thesis presumes first that ideas and studies about male and female relationships during slavery have been misconstrued or misrepresented and second that resistance to enslavement was a cooperative enterprise rather than solitary male behavior. In spite of the professor's rejection, Ursa always planned to conduct a self-directed study. In part, *Daughters* itself, in the form of a novel about male and female cooperative political venture, becomes that proposed investigation.

Estelle and Primus's common goals for the community, at least initially, and their work toward these goals epitomize an inherited legacy of resistance. After Primus has been in government for twenty years, the young politician campaigning to unseat him does so with the aid of Primus's wife. Nonetheless, *Daughters* suggests that egalitarian community-focused activity between partners has been jeopardized. The men seem more easily seduced by interests ultimately antithetical to those of the community. In Midland City, for example, the African-American mayor supports the highway to suburbia, while Mae Ryland, who had worked tirelessly for his election, retrenches herself in the community. In Triunion, Primus endorses a project that will divest the islanders of prime beach property, but Estelle subverts the project to preserve the cultural integrity of the community and to prevent their exploitation by Western investors. The man who might have been the complementary Cudjoe figure to Ursa's Jane refuses to leave a job that he hates and that is splintering his spirit. In Brooklyn, Ursa's friend

Viney combats the institutionalized violence of the police department directed toward the emasculation of black boys and toward her son in particular. *Daughters* suggests that resistance against oppression in its various guises has fallen primarily on the shoulders of women. Such a state of affairs signifies the reversal of historic practice and an immeasurable loss of human resources, both of which are critical to the sustenance of black communities.

Marshall signifies these ruptured relationships and the abysmal loss of potential in personal and communal arenas through the use of abortion as metaphor. Abortion receives thematic and structural narrative significance from three strategic women, all linked in one way or another to Primus Mackenzie and to Triunion and to U.S. cities. The Astral Forde's abortion demonstrates the lost potential of poor island women exploited through gender and class. Her example suggests that there is minimal or no opportunity for woman's financial autonomy except through the intercession a man who then expects sexual favors in return. The violence of the exploitation, articulated through Astral's rape by a boy from a dance, reinforces the power structure and recalls the rape of the mare in the MacKenzie yard: Astral's date/attacker initially enters her from the rear. Subsequently, her abortion, crudely performed, leaves her feeling as if the wire has been left inside. Astral's various lovers before Primus all help her advance in the work world, but she must compensate them with her body.

Unlike Astral, whose abortion is clinically induced, Estelle naturally aborts several fetuses. As the character most affected by Primus's betrayal of his principles, her numerous "slides" (the island women's description for the body's natural expulsion of a fetus) portend Estelle's gradual disenchantment with her husband and the instability of political affairs on the island. Her enthusiasm, originally fueled by knowledge of a history of resistance on the island, dwindles and shrinks like the aborted fetuses or like the piles of overripe fruit abandoned at the market. Estelle's and Primus's potential for realizing their heritage of resistance is only minimally activated because of Primus's self-contradictions.

Ursa's abortion in a fancy New York clinic, the first event in the

novel, introduces the subject as a motif. Positioned against her deteriorating relationship with her boyfriend, Carruthers, and her childhood
memories of her father, her abortion signifies loss, rejection, and disappointment in intimate relationships and in broader contexts. Carruthers's diatribe about his job has become insufferable, as has her
unverbalized disillusionment with her father's static politics in Triunion, where social and economic problems persist. Ursa's abortion—
its emptiness and loss—also encompasses the discarded potential of
Carruthers, whose work is sucking out his spirit, turning him into a
raging monomaniac. Ursa resigns her prestigious position for a lowly
service job, but Carruthers refuses to work where he would prefer, with
black youth in the service sector.

Ironically, Ursa's abortion prefigures her severance from emotional
bondage to her father. Although her disillusionment with him has been
manifested by her refusal to visit the island, her discovery of his com-
plicitous behavior in the beach scheme brings her disappointment to a
climax. Exposing his plan to his opponent represents rebellion in the
tradition of Congo Jane, rather than betrayal, but Ursa acts without a
counterpart for Will Cudjoe. Instead, Estelle, another woman, exposes
Primus's duplicity to Ursa; consequently, Ursa informs her father's
political opponent of the PM's betrayal of his contituency. In privileg-
ing the community and resisting oppression in the attractive disguise
of a resort, both women perpetuate the legacy of Congo Jane and Will
Cudjoe.

Paradoxically, Ursa's rebellious act against her father enables the
onset of her liberation as if it were a metaphorical completion of the
abortion three months earlier. Her revelation exorcises her father's stifling influence. She achieves emotional liberation, which connects her
with the spirit of community and the legacy of female political resistance. Ursa's example reaffirms the value of individual service to the
community over many other concerns.

Judith Newton points out that feminist criticism seeks to "change
the world." She poses the question of the "relationship of literature and
therefore of literary criticism to the real conditions of our lives" (124).
Literary texts are read "as gestures toward history and gestures with

political effect. . . . We speak of making our model of literary criticism, choosing to see in it not an ostensibly objective reading of a text but an act of political intervention, a mode of shaping the cultural use to which women's writing and men's will be put. [Therefore, we resist the] view that literature and literature critics are divorced from history" (124).

Newton's reflective approach to the integration of literature with culture and history is essential for thinking about the responsibilities and relationships discussed in texts like *Daughters*. Neither *Daughters* nor other Marshall novels falls into a category of support for the authority of any imperial center. Rather, her works demand a reading that radically questions relationships between power and historicity. *Daughters* insists that the spectator assume an interior penetration that deconstructs ruling class power in formerly colonized countries and questions the Third World status of black communities in the First World. Theory that is responsive to texts like *Daughters* must therefore mesh with discourses of decolonization.

The Pernicious Triad: The Dynamics of Race, Class, and Gender in the Quest for Wholeness

Racism has done serious damages to the psyches of all people. Whether one observes the Untouchables of Asia, the dark-skinned people of Europe and America or the Blacks and "coloreds" of South Afrika, the common battle fought by all of them on a daily basis is one of survival, and development in a world that judges and categorizes them first and foremost, by the pigmentation of their skin. —Haki Madhubuti

The Necessity of Survival

Surviving is a critical dimension of life in the fiction of Paule Marshall. Both male and female characters almost always have the motivation essential for survival; unfortunately, they are not always victorious against the potent conspiracy of forces arrayed against them. Marshall's black characters understand the role of race in their survival strategies. Their behavior suggests that they understand the concept of class as well, since, for some of them, upward social and economic mobility becomes their consuming ambition. Many of them, like Silla and Deighton Boyce in *Brownstones*, Jerome Johnson in *Praisesong*, or Merle Kinbona in *The Chosen Place*, talk about the social constructs that endanger their economic survival. In such conversations, they express their suspicion of how these constructs impede psychic survival and deter spiritual wholeness. Marshall's characters illustrate the intricacies in the confluence of race, class, and gender that perpetuate the conditions and environments that create the fractured psyche.

Oppression for black men has long been attributed to race and class. At one time, discussion of the problems of black men was assumed to include the problems of black women. Recent scholarship, however, has identified double and multiple oppressions that have historically beset black women and that can in most cases be traced to the dynamics of race, class, and gender. Feminists, womanists, sociologists, historians, and writers, among others, recognize the internecine capability of this triad. Isolating the relationships among them and the absence of spiritual wholeness are essential to any study that examines strategies of survival among black men and women.

Since the 1960s much gender research has focused on black women. Bonnie Thornton Dill affirms a broad complex of forces that define characterizing trends for black women both collectively and individually (548). Similarly, Deborah K. King argues that "racism, sexism, and classism constitute three interdependent control systems" that she terms "multiple" in reference "not only to several, simultaneous oppressions but to the multiplicative relationships among them as well" (47). Patricia Hill Collins has also determined that "ideologies of race and gender converge in explaining African American social class position" ("Social Constructions," 882). Zillah Eisenstein establishes vital connections among gender, race, and class and the delineation and the apportionment of power, arguing that a woman's existence is managed by "the relations of power which shape her activity and the ideology which defines, protects, and maintains it" (20). Gloria Wade-Gayles emphasizes, however, "a clear understanding of race and sex in black women's reality" (7), while Paula Giddings views race as "still the salient issue" for black women in terms of occupational and educational gains in the past forty years (350).

The objective world through which men and women move in Marshall's fiction is most assuredly one where the consequences of gender, race, and class are readily apparent. The dialectics that determine their places as men and women of color, how much (if any) power they exercise, and whether they may expect any degree of social progression is circumscribed by these dynamics. Her fiction, in embodying these disabling and often destructive forces, inscribes a context for envisioning, examining, and understanding these double and multiple oppressions. It confirms their configurations as the source of oppressions.

Characters in Marshall's fiction experience the problems traditionally attributed to race, among them, low-paying jobs for men, domestic and factory work for women, backbreaking field labor in the Caribbean, segregated communities, racial insults, feelings of alienation from the prevailing culture, and powerlessness. The concept of race is pervasive in their response to the world, a constant in their interpretation of the world's interaction with them. In *Brown Girl* the reality of racism epitomizes one of the rites of passage to adulthood for Selina Boyce. In her encounter with a white dancer's mother, wearing the tight smile of friendliness, the woman's eyes "were a well-lighted mirror in which, for the first time, Selina truly saw—with a sharp and shattering clarity— the full meaning of her black skin" (289). Racism is almost as devastating in its ability to erode a secure self. Selina's encounter is not merely an issue of personal acceptance, but a perception of the devaluation of blackness within American society. After her epiphany, Selina knows the worst: her dark face must be confused in their minds with what they feared most, the night, a symbol of ancient fears that seethed with sin and harbored violence (291). Her wound is psychic, whereas the never healed wound on the foot of her elderly friend, Miss Thompson, incurred because of race and gender (resistance to sexual aggression), is both emotional and physical and exemplifies the pervasiveness of racism in both the South and North. The juxtaposed experiences of Selina and Miss Thompson need not be as strikingly replicated in Marshall's later texts to communicate the longevity and psychic scarring of racism. It exists, as constant as air.

Race figures prominently in male survival in Marshall's fiction. Rendered in striking complexity, the men illustrate a variety of methods of responding to the power of the dominant culture. What happens to them suggests the many ways in which race and class control their lives. Since Marshall's communities encompass the Caribbean, South America, and the United States, she shows that the effects of race defy circumscription by geographical boundaries. Her male characters' identity and self-esteem are constantly jeopardized by continuous covert and overt assaults on their psyches during the workday. They mistakenly believe that economic improvement will cause others to perceive them better, substituting class status for race. Thus, they work multiple jobs to facilitate economic mobility. This profile fits Deighton Boyce, Percy Challenor, and Mr. Springer in *Brown Girl*; Jerome Johnson in *Praisesong*; Vere in *The Chosen Place*; and Mr. Watford in "Barbados" in *Soul Clap Hands and Sing*.

The Failure of Male Survival in *Soul Clap Hands and Sing*

> Society, it would seem, is a flimsy structure, beneath contempt,
>
> designed by and for all the other people, and experience is nothing
>
> more than sensation . . . added up like arithmetic [to] give one the
>
> rich full life. They thus lose what it was they so bravely set out to
>
> find, their own personalities, which having been deprived of all
>
> nourishment soon ceast, in effect, to exist.—James Baldwin

Marshall warns her readers through her selection of an excerpt from William B. Yeats's poem, "Sailing to Byzantium," that the common bonds among the four novellas that comprise *Soul Clap Hands and Sing* will be gender and the absence of spiritual wholeness: "An aged man is but a paltry thing / A tattered coat upon a stick, unless / Soul clap its hands and sing." These lines signify the unifying focus, a male protagonist in confrontation with his static and unrealized potential in the autumn of his life. Age and spiritual emptiness thematically unify the novellas, but varying circumstances have led four men in different geographical regions to the same juncture. Each protagonist has neglected to embrace the fullness of life when he was younger, and each one discovers his inability to recapture what he has lost, although each one feebly attempts to do so. Each novella confirms that life possesses the joyous capacity for spiritual life, for connectedness to other people, and for a satisfying sense of individuation. The ability and desire to achieve these states are interior, psychological processes not always easily analyzed. If, in part or whole, they are unrealized, only then does man (or woman) become in old age "a paltry thing / A tattered coat upon a stick," an empty shell of a human being, pitiable in self-wrought loneliness. In these stories, Marshall encompasses more than Yeats's image of an old and empty human being; she explores the character's responsibility for his hollow state and his shock of recognition upon that realization. Because she focuses on the spiritual emptiness of old men while the women survive, this early novella is especially interesting for what it portends for the author's developing vision.

In "Barbados," seventy-year-old Mr. Watford returns to Barbados to purchase and operate a coconut farm after fifty years of exile in Boston, where he had achieved economic security. In "Brooklyn," Max Berman, a Jew, a teacher of thirty years, teaches French literature in a small college in Brooklyn, trying to salvage a career that has been destroyed because of his Communist Party membership. In "British Guiana," the longest story, Gerald Motley, born in British Guiana but educated in England, has been back home for forty years. He is the only protagonist consciously affected by the knowledge of his diverse racial strands and what they mean in the composition of his life. In "Brazil," the last story of the collection, O Grande Caliban, retiring as a comedian after thirty-five years of stage appearances in Rio, cannot distinguish his public persona from his private self, Heitor Baptista Guimares. All of these men, deficient in their own estimations, attempt to compensate for or to ameliorate their conditions through interaction with women. All of these men, Darwin Turner says, incorporate the weaknesses of modernity, deficiencies not limited to one race or country (introduction to *Soul Clap Hands and Sing*, xlvi).

In "Barbados" and "Brooklyn," the two novellas most often excerpted from this collection, Mr. Watford and Max Berman, respectively, attempt to delay their deaths by wrestling the spirit of life from young black women. Ironically, the women have recently experienced a resurgence of spiritual life caused, in part, by their interactions with Watford and Berman, whose efforts they spurn. The deft strokes with which character is drawn in "Barbados" typify Marshall's ability to convey depth; subtle distinctions between characters enhance their contrasting approaches to life. Eliminating a first name for Mr. Watford, even among his closest acquaintances, for example, distances him philosophically and spiritually from his community. Watford never addresses the boy or the girl who interact with him by name, thus enforcing and confirming the dissociation and alienation that prefigure his spiritual moribundity. "The girl," to whom Watford appeals to save himself, is described in one passage as "standing in his driveway, her bare feet like strong dark roots amid the jagged stones, her face tilted toward the sun. . . . She seemed of the sun, of the earth . . . rich and black and warmed by the sun. . . . [She wore] a sober brown felt hat which should have been worn by some stout English matron in a London suburb. . . . Below her waist, her hips branched wide, the place prepared for its load of life. But it was the bold and sensual strength of her legs which completely unstrung Mr. Watford" (15). The girl's naturalness and proper balance, her propensity to give life and to accept love are succinctly conveyed. When images of rootedness and balance occur in Marshall's texts, they anchor a character to earth and indicate either a strong potential for wholeness or a spiritually balanced character.

Mr. Watford's Spartan existence and rigid routines, both in Barbados and during the fifty years in Boston, have deprived him of a meaningful love relationship and a family (7). His recognition that such a relationship can redirect the deathward thrust of his life and displace its loneliness motivates his offering himself to the new female servant.

Coming after his harsh rejection of her thin offer of companionship, he is too late, however, and the girl condemns him as inhuman: "You ain't people, Mr. Watford, you ain't people!" (27). The girl's presence in his house, however, engenders his recognition of the void that has characterized his existence. Mr. Watford "would have confessed that it had been love, terrible in its demand, which he had always fled. . . . [He] had not been willing to bear the weight of his own responsibility" (26).

Like Watford, Max Berman reaches age sixty-three without the memory of love, although he has been married twice. Like the other men in *Soul Clap Hands and Sing*, Berman encounters self-knowledge when he attempts to exploit a young black female student. His life has been marked by indifference and lack of commitment since his boyhood. His recognition of Miss Williams's loneliness as she sits in his French class and of the history of suffering of black people, which tie them together results in his plan for her seduction rather than in any confraternity between them. Berman confronts, however, the imminence of his death as Miss Williams demonstrates her embracing of life.

Like the servant girl in "Barbados," natural images connect Miss Williams to the earth. When she laughs as Berman shows her the woods surrounding his house, the sound "joined her, it seemed, to the wood and wide fields, to the hills; she shared their simplicity and held within her the same strong current of life" (55). Ironically, Williams's parents had directed her toward a life of noninvolvement that would translate into the indifference that characterized Berman's existence. Their rationalization, to protect her from black people darker than she was and from the racism of white people, resulted in enforced loneliness and in denial of life's pleasures. The interaction with Max, however, has demonstrated that there is no safety and certainly no life in spiritual isolation. Berman's feeble effort at exploitation serves as a catalyst that spurs her subdued anger and quiet rage into defiance of him and the limitations that her parents imposed. Her rejection of his offer is a rejection of gender victimization. As important, Williams has seized life, "something vital and purposeful and precious, which she [has] found and [guards] like a prize within her center" (60). In contrast, Max tragically accepts the impossibility of wrestling this spark of life from her and takes responsibility for the dismal trajectory of his life.

Gerald Motley in "British Guiana" never accepts responsibility for the stasis that impedes his life. Instead, he remains ensnared in the malaise that results from the conflicted state of public identity that undermines his self-identity. In "British Guiana" and "Brazil," in fact, the male protagonists confront the issues of identity and class differently. The name Motley reflects Gerald's heterogeneous European, black, and East Indian racial heritage. "He was all these strains, yet no one singly, and because of this he was called in B.G. creole or colored—*highcolored*. His family had once been modestly wealthy and very proud" (70). Motley's malaise is linked to his indeterminacy about his identity. His uncertainty is reflected in his cynicism and joking self-debasement and in his assertion that he is British Guiana, that he comprises the complexities of the place inseparable from its history. His uncertainty is also reinforced by his surname, which also means having many colors. But *motley* also refers to the professional attire of a court jester. Although Motley's professional attire in the heat of a tropical setting— a white linen suit and Panama hat—reflects his occupation in broadcast journalism and thus his public image, it makes an ironic comment, given his confusion about his private identity and his behavioral contradictions of his public image. And like the court jester of Shakespeare's dramas, Motley serves as the receptacle for satire, cynicism, and verbal abuse by Sidney Parrish, a young dark-skinned reporter Motley hired at the station who is Motley's alter ego.

"I am B.G.," Motley proclaims to his drinking cronies in the bar. " 'We're one and the same.' He [knew] suddenly that what he had sought all along had been the reflection of himself in each feature of the land" (99).[1] His human community is connected in spite of racial, ethnic, gender, political, social, and economic barriers, although the consistent rejection and artificial partions erected among these affinities erode them. Motley thus becomes Marshall's initial exploration of interrelations among character, culture, and place, a voyage that culminates in the protagonist of *The Chosen Place*, Merle Kinbona, who embodies more severely Motley's psychological displacement and identity problems in British Guiana.

The persistency of race and color issues as the legacy of slavery, their exacerbation during colonization by Spain, Britain, France, and the Netherlands, and the migration of East Indians, Japanese, and Chinese to the islands in the nineteenth century comprise Gerald Motley's fragmentation. Sociologists and historians studying the Caribbean identify rigid social and economic structures held in place by race and color. This pattern placed a minority of whites at the top, divided by wealth, education, and occupation. Slaves and their descendants were at the opposite end, while a mixed, colored section occupied the middle. The coloreds sometimes received preferential treatment and acquired positions that could result in prestige, though they lacked social equality to whites (Hoetink, 77, 69). This legacy shapes Motley, thus making the historical circumstances that underlie racial mixtures in descendants of Africans, particularly in the Caribbean, inseparable from problems of identity, race, class, and gender.

In Marshall's exposure of the factors that exacerbate identity, multiple racial strands hinder the ability to reach individuation. While Motley's acceptance of a creole identity guarantees social acceptibility, it undermines his spiritual wholeness. Although he receives the British education, serves as program director at the local radio station, owns an imported Jaguar, and occupies a large house on an acceptable street, he has become disillusioned and hollow because he has denied the racial heritage that would have been most problematic, the Afro-Caribbean strand. Motley's victimization is historically inflicted, but it is self-perpetuated. His emptiness is largely the result of his inability or refusal to confront his true identity and to separate his self from the multiple strands that compose him. Curiously, he blames his thwarted moment on his lover, Sybil Jeffries, "a part-Chinese Negro girl from a village outside Georgetown," who is educated and was the first colored reporter for the newspaper (71, 84). In the interior of the island, Motley's moment of prescience is thwarted by Sybil:

The bush had closed around him, becoming another dimension of himself, the self he had long sought. For the first time this self was within his grasp . . . and it would either shape his life by giving him the right answer to Orly's offer [of the broadcasting job] or destroy him. . . .

[Sybil] might have been the sane and cautious part of himself coming to save him. . . . She clearly saw what he had only glimpsed and understood better than he ever would its danger. . . . [She] placed herself between him and *what could have been a vision of himself.* (emphasis added, 75)

Gerald Motley has three choices for his racial identity: he could "pass" in England or the United States; he could embrace his African heritage, which would mean expulsion from the prestige he enjoys in his community; or he could embrace his creole identity. He selects the third option. Perhaps more important that any particular racial identity, Motley rejects his inner calling. He had once attempted to lead the stevedores in a strike against the powerful British monopoly Orly Shipping Ltd., and just a year after marrying the "fair-complexioned daughter of a highly respected Georgetown family," had begun an affair with Sybil Jeffries. The proximity of the job offer to the attempted strike and to the trip into the bush during which his crucial self-discovery is thwarted is more than coincidental.

If Sybil really obstructed Motley's vision of his self in the bush, what he might have seen would have been more devastating than the hollow man that he became. He would have confronted the darkness of his racial biases and his rejection of African heritage for the social and economic benefits of descendency from the East Indians and British. He would have perceived his deficiency in confronting the loneliness that Sybil brings to their encounters, which he is helpless in assuaging. He would have been forced to acknowledge that he would never be spiritually whole. He would have glimpsed, perhaps, the consequences of his choice of a public identity—his fragmentation, his loneliness, his excessive drinking, his lack of meaningful work, and even the change in his sexual orientation. Dorothy Dennison perceptively connects Mot-

ley's "multi-cultural and multi-racial background . . . with his confusion about his bi-sexuality . . . [as] a stagnating form of psychological
repression. Repressing values and natural tendencies become paradig-
matic of the country itself" (210).

Motley's remote anger and cynicism at his complicity in his own
exploitation by the system finds appropriate representation through
Sidney Parrish, the announcer who functions as Motley's alter ego.
Parrish's insolence and sharp verbal assaults are as essential to Motley
as the mind-numbing alcohol that he consumes to assuage his self-
loathing. Parrish's anger at the system in British Guiana keeps him
alive, at least temporarily, while Motley's complicity has signaled his
death. Thus, the many references to death in the story—Parrish's daily
announcement of deaths in the district, for example—are not superflu-
ous. Instead they signify Motley's living-in-death state and the same
potential for Sidney.

Motley's potential female rescuer, Sybil, offers salvation through a
job at the Jamaican radio station where she works. Pride and the truth of
his deficiencies compel his cynical response—loud, irreverent, hollow
laughter—to this epiphany, because he bluntly perceives an irretriev-
able self-loss. Thus, he is spiritually dead before his physical demise the
same night.

The dynamics of identity, gender, and class that shape the action
in "British Guiana" reappear with a different twist in "Brazil," where
O Grande Caliban's identity search foregrounds the conflict that arises
because he does not know himself. After thirty-five years as a nightclub
comedian, O Grande Caliban has been "everyman, so much so that it
had become difficult . . . to separate out of the welter of faces he could
assume his face, to tell where O Grande Caliban ended and he, Heitor
Baptista Guimares began" (134). Caliban's impending retirement is the
catalyst for thinking about his other self because without his comedy
shows, no audience will validate and celebrate the Caliban identity. His
public persona has fully effaced the private self (even his new wife
and Miranda, his assistant, do not know the name "Heitor Guimares").
Marilyn Nelson Waniek identifies his movement from one social class
to another—from a peasant to a wealthy, respected, "whiter" person—

as a reason for the identity loss (53). Confronting this fact, Caliban literally searches for someone who remembers Heitor ("the name of a stranger who had lived at another time" [152]), as if that person would provide adequate confirmation of his other self. His futile search results in his acknowledgment that after retirement, "he would be left without a self" (175).

Although Caliban's literal search for Heitor Guimares takes him back to the old section of Rio where he had long ago worked in a restaurant, his journey does not become the quest Marshall develops in later fiction. In fact, his failure to discover himself occurs because his search is exterior; he expects others to provide knowledge, but identity must emanate from within. Moreover, his fame as Caliban has disconnected him from a community, except as a figure of fortune. When he travels to the slums above Rio, the favela, he brings the flashy trappings of the city, making him incongruous with the squalor there, and self-discovery becomes impossible. "His eye passed quickly over the ugliness there: it was too much a reminder of what he had known" (164).

Unlike the other men in these novellas, Caliban is not womanless as he approaches his crisis of identity and old age. He has married and impregnated a twenty-five-year-old and thus might have assured his protection against the hollowness of old age. The innocent young woman from Caliban's village, however, has been attracted to him because of his visibility as a performer and the chance to live in Rio. She is ignorant of his other identity and helpless in his quest. However, the second woman in Caliban's life, his stage partner, is more pertinent to his journey. Marshall conflates several identities and images through Caliban's union with his assistant. Their physical and ethnic incongruity, from which much of the comedy of their act has emerged, becomes the means through which Marshall exacts multiple meanings for Caliban's problem of identity. As Lloyd Brown has pointed out, both Miranda and Caliban are enmeshed in the "socio-sexual roles which dominate their culture and which they reenact on-stage" (165). In spite of his small physical stature, the culture demands his domination of the woman although she is large and literally lifts and carries him as part of their act. Brown views her tactics as a means of compensating for her lack of authority in society by manipulating whatever insecurity her superior possesses. Marshall undermines the roles of dominance and subjugation suggested in their routine, however, based on the reality of their ethnic differences—Caliban is a dark-skinned Brazillian, and Miranda is a tall, statuesque German. Caliban's stage role as diminutive boxing champion is comic. His role is feigned domination and Miranda's is feigned subjugation. In a similar vein Marshall draws upon the name recognition of Caliban and Miranda from Shakespeare's *The Tempest*. Caliban, of course, evokes the "brute" in contrast to Miranda's refinement (Talbert, 55).

Caliban equates Miranda's glass-and-white apartment with the city of Rio and sees himself reflected in both as a "tiny dog, who lent the room an amusing touch but had no real place there. . . . The abundance of white throughout stripped him of importance, denied him all significance" (171). This perception forces his unarticulated discovery that his identity as Heitor Guimares has been usurped by an impersonal city, symbolized by the heterogeneous nightclub audiences that have fueled his Caliban identity, but the spectators will now discard and forget him. Thus, his destruction of Miranda's apartment signifies his rage at a city that allows him only the identity of a clown, a physically inconsequential dark-skinned man who plays to a "startlingly tall, long-limbed woman with white skin that appear[s] luminous in the spotlight and blond hair piled like whipped cream" (132). Miranda's cry of "meu negrinho" at the story's end, in effect calling Caliban "my Negro child," confirms that at bottom, in spite of their stage and personal relationship, her image of him has been the stereotypical one. Even after his display of brutish behavior in destroying her apartment, an extension of the stage performance of the diminutive boxer, he is less than an adult male in her eyes, in the eyes of the audience. Thus, his discovery undermines even his Caliban identity, illustrating its vacuousness and dependency on parodied stereotype.

Spiritual wholeness has eluded these early male characters in Marshall's canon, thus reducing them in old age to empty, hollow beings, nothing more than stick figures. That is all they might be without spiritual wholeness to bind up their fractured selves, infusing them with the desire to clap hands and sing. But they have been the agents of their own spiritual demise in a multiplicity of ways until it is too late for their reclamation. Although the women might have become their rescuers, what happens in Marshall's fiction suggests that individual vision and communal attachment, essential to binding fracturing, must come from within.

Ethnicity and Symbols of Capitalism

> Throw the whole lot in together, I say. And they all usually come,
>
> even though, of course, each group keeps to itself. You'll see.
>
> Class! It's a curse upon us. —*The Chosen Place*

Race, class, and gender are constructs of a capitalist patriarchy, and, as such, they become useful divisions for exploitation. "Some Marxists have even contended that race exploitation is simply class exploitation. . . . For them racial exploitation is a species of class exploitation, but they do not believe that the converse is true" (McGary, 20). Marxist feminists, however, specifically identify capitalism or class oppression as the first-order offender.[2]

Marshall's fiction illustrates how race, class, and gender oppressions dovetail and overlap and how they are inseparable from the world of work and capitalist profit. Her characters' fates suggest that industrialization is antithetical to spiritual and physical survival for nonwhite workers. The industrialized Western world elevates commodities and profit over the human being and in so doing doubly oppresses nonwhite workers—triply if they are nonwhite and female. The labor of people of color is more likely to involve drudgery and to exact physical toil. Relegating many people of African descent to the lowest and most physically exacting labor constitutes racist behavior that collides with class, even manipulates it, because under- or low-paid workers, male and female, then comprise an underclass and to some extent a middle class. This black middle class defines itself differently from the middle class of the dominant culture.[3] When women enter the equation, gender oppression becomes an issue, particularly if the history of black women in industry is accurately represented. One could argue that the emphasis on exposing these interlocking social constructs in Marshall's fiction is intended to advance a socioeconomic critique in a politically astute way. Her representation of race, class, and gender oppressions conflates her development of spiritual deprivation in people of African descent with her sociocultural critique.

The machinery of industry epitomizes the destructive capabilities of capitalism in the United States and in the Caribbean, where the British-controlled sugar industry at one time constituted the primary capitalist enterprise. For this reason, the sugarcane farmers on Bourne island in *The Chosen Place* refuse to use tools or participate in the "government schemes" designed to ameliorate Third World economic conditions: pipes for the irrigation system lie rusting in the small cane fields; a factory intended for pottery production decays because people refuse to work there; an experimental banana grove intended eventually to replace small cane plots fails for lack of participation.

The rationale for the villagers' nonparticipation—poor planning or lack of village involvement—nevertheless leaves the "feeling that something apart from the obvious had also been at play" (157). Intuitively, perhaps, the men and women understand that economic assistance from the West to Third World countries, in whatever its guise, will ultimately extend the exploitation already in place. Perhaps these subsistence producers remain in the reactionary mode because they know that "at its most powerful, colonialism is a process of radical dispossession" (Deane, 10). Thus, within the structures of British colonialism that persist in spite of formal independence, the workers continue as they are, biding their time until solutions evolve from within their own cultures.

The exploitation and the sense of static time are evoked in the narrative of *The Chosen Place* through the sugarcane industry. For example, Marshall describes the factory, called Cane Vale, in the imagery of a slave ship, emphasizing its connection to British patriarchy through the "smokestack rising above it like a great phallus" (154). The noise of the cane-crushing rollers is "shrill, almost [a] human wail"; the light was "dim and murky as in the hold of a ship"; the workers appeared almost disembodied, "ghosts . . . from some long sea voyage taken centuries ago" (154).

Other passages detailing the daily work of the islanders recall conditions of forced and uncompensated labor, including an overseer (estate manager) patrolling the fields on a horse, maintaining the structure of a bygone era. The process of cutting, gathering, tying, and heading the canes in monstrous heat to waiting trucks seems designed for beasts of burden.[4] Saul Amron observes that the cane-cutting process has "a feel of unreality, of something taking place at a time long passed" (161). Images of ghosts and the dead perpetuate the concept of stalled time, as if the workers are ghosts of slaves, constrained to continue in the same manner despite legal emancipation. The cutter Stinger's body, for example, appeared to be "shriveled bones and muscles within the drawn sac of skin and the one arm flailing away with a mind and will of its own" (162). And the eyes of Stinger's wife, Gwen, had the "slightly turned up, fixed, flat stare that you find upon drawing back the lids of someone asleep or dead" (163). This backbreaking labor barely allows the most meager survival. The cane rollers at Cane Vale have literally killed Leesy Wilkes's husband, who fell from the platform into the pit, but the work kills the human spirit as well, as indicated in the descriptions of Stinger and his wife.

The treachery of industrialization and its value system is not confined by geographic region; Marshall characterizes industrialization's deleterious effects on the body and spirit in *Brown Girl* through the mangling of Deighton Boyce's arm in a factory accident. Silla Boyce's movements, however, rhythmically attuned with the machines where she works, signify her spiritual seduction by and embracing of capitalist ideology, which offers the same consequences to workers in the lower echelons in New York and in the West Indies. Selina, Deighton and Silla's daughter, reimagines the scene, however, as "the huge hungry maw of the machine opening while her father tended it absently. . . . It clamped down on his arm, sucking it . . . then spewing it out crushed. . . . And thinking of that impersonal brutality, she wept" (155).

Similarly, Selina observes (literally) her mother's accord with machinery after black women are hired for factory work during World War II. Silla is similarly comfortable working at her stove. "Like the others, her movements were attuned to the mechanical rhythms of the machine-mass. . . . Only the mother's own formidable force could match that of the machines; only the mother could remain indifferent to the brutal noise" (99).

Gender, class, and assimilation converge in this discussion of Deighton and Silla. Silla's rapport with the machinery demonstrates her acceptance of Western values, while Deighton's mangling graphically symbolizes the spiritual injury enacted upon him and others like him.[5] His ambivalence as a West Indian immigrant is consistent with David Reimers's research in *Still the Golden Door: The Third World Comes to America*; some West Indians intended to labor in the United States only long enough to acquire savings and then to return home (3). Deighton's example is highly problematic: He cannot achieve his personal standard for manhood, one based on the images in the systems that oppress him as a male of color. He also cannot prosper through economics that restrict him to an underclass. His image of manhood rejects the concept of patience during years of meager accumulation. His devaluation in the system that privileges the white male of economic means, however, has already occurred. He has been "utterly unmanned . . . before he was yet a man; they had stripped him of any possibility of self and then hustled him out" (182). Incapable of articulating this devaluation and loss of self, he instead swathes himself in romantic buoyancy and self-defensiveness as he belittles Silla's economic goals and patience and envisions himself surpassing them.

Thus, Deighton's character is simultaneously attracted to yet repelled by assimilation. In Brooklyn, his behavior indicates compliance with cultural assimilation, for example, when he decries the smell of codfish on his clothing, "the indisputable sign that he was Barbadian and a foreigner" (22). Economically, like Silla, he wants the rewards of hard labor—a home and material possessions for his daughter. But his plans to return to the Caribbean undermine the perception of him as completely emeshed by the American dream, like his wife and the rest of the Barbadian community. Moreover, Deighton is a dreamer and romantic rather than a realist, like his wife. His impatience drives him to economic quick fixes, to enrollment in home courses such as accounting, radio repair, and trumpet playing.

The examples of Silla and Deighton Boyce suggest that seduction by Western values must be absolute, like that of Silla and the other Barba-

dians. There is no space within the system for workers to earn enough
for economic sustenance yet still maintain the appropriate aloofness to
safeguard spiritual heartiness. Thus, Deighton's rejection of the economic goals of his wife and of his West Indian community invites their
scorn and his ejection from the group. Significantly, the rejection occurs
at a wedding dance, a community ritual that symbolizes life's continuity
and echoes the group's African heritage: "The men at the bar [and] the
dancers turned in one body and danced with their backs to him. . . .
[Their] dark contemptuous faces charged him. Those eyes condemned
him and their voices rushed full tilt at him . . . driving him from
their presence" (150). Deighton's crushed arm signifies his rejection
by the capitalistic system. Joining a religious movement, a temporary
panacea that allows his psychic wounds to submerge, precedes his suicide when he is deported by immigration authorities. Silla's function in
her husband's deportation can be explained from the perspective of her
alignment with capitalist ideology.

Silla's philosophy of economic power and her survival signal her
compatibility with the system, thus enabling her physical survival but
impairing her spiritual wholeness, which incorporates compassion for
community. Silla's philosophy embraces the Western value of elevating
the individual over the group: "And nearly always to make your way
in this Christ world you got to be hard and sometimes misuse others,
even your own" (224). "People got a right to claw their way to the top
and those on top got a right to scuffle to stay there. . . . Power is a
thing that don't make you nice" (225). Selina rejects the system that
her mother and her Barbadian community have adopted, defining its
ugliness as follows: "It's the result of living by the most shameful codes
possible—dog eat dog, exploitation, the strong over the weak, the end
justifies the means—the whole kit and caboodle" (227).

Capitalism, which translates into economic success for Silla and the
like-minded Barbadian community, is also a means of class elevation
for Percy Challenor and Mr. Springer, minor characters in the novel.
Unlike Deighton, they survive in and learn to manipulate the system to
meet their economic goals. Although they share Silla's objectives, they
succeed more quickly than she.

The difference of gender as a barometer in the realization of economic goals is pertinent. Silla's experiences and those of other women in the text—Miss Thompson and Suggie, for example—are typical of the intricate dynamics between class and gender, even in same-race situations. Silla's and Suggie's realities parallel Deborah King's finding that class status for black women constitutes "an autonomous source of persecution," since many of them experience the lowest wages and worst conditions of rural and urban poverty (46). The employment of Silla and Suggie as domestics seems a "recapitulation [of] the mistress-slave relationship" (Jones, 127). Silla tolerates the menial labor as a means to an end, only thinking of the " 'few raw mout' pennies at the end of the day which would eventually buy house" (11). To upgrade her economic class, Silla also rents out rooms in the brownstone and deceives her husband to sell his land in Barbados. Suggie, however, seems more to parallel Deighton in her response to capitalism. She, too, works in the factory but neither maintains the job nor shares the economic goals of her fellow Bajans. Silla ejects her as a boarder in the brownstone as she rejected Deighton, because, like him, Suggie is unfit for self-sacrifice in the name of materialism. In spite of Silla's efforts, her economic progress lags behind that of male Bajans because domestic work offered low wages and was the primary nonprofessional employment for women until munitions factories hired black women during World War II.[6]

Marshall's characters illustrate the unlikelihood of spiritual rapprochement for people who are mindlessly captivated by the allure of materialism and enticed by Western values antithetical to their cultural properties. The author frequently appropriates symbols of Western industrialization to suggest the disruption perpetrated on unsuspecting populations. The Bentley automobile that Merle Kinbona drives in *The Chosen Place*, for example, is obviously a symbol of the prestige and authority accorded to the most representative figure of imperialism and colonialism on the island, the governor. By the time Merle drives the car, however, it has been reduced to a shell of its former stateliness. It is as if she has vented her rage at the inequities of the system against the car: "It appeared to have been deliberately abused, willfully desecrated. Someone, perhaps the woman herself, might have taken a sledge hammer and battered in the huge front fenders which swept forward with all the controlled drama of a wave curving in on itself, then scraped off the black paint from the body in great ugly patches that resembled sores, and, as a final insult, driven it head-on into a wall, caving in the high grill that was its trademark" (4).

In other instances, capitalist symbols actively participate in the physical destruction of characters already spiritually moribund. Gerald Motley, for example, having acknowledged his hollowness, dies when his Jacguar automobile crashes.

Marshall most arrestingly demonstrates how the industrialized West can exploit in the character of Vereson Walkes, called Vere, a young man in *The Chosen Place* who leaves Bournehills to work for three years harvesting cane in Florida.[7] Vere's terse description of his experience implies its affinity with slavery without specifying details: isolation in barracks, poor food, exposure to extreme heat and cold, severe bosses, and a contract that in effect enslaves the workers. He returns to Bournehills with "scarred and swollen" hands and a prematurely hardened body, turned out "with a parting gift of an outdated slickster's hat, suit and shoes" (30).[8]

Vere's experiences in Florida as part of a government work plan for West Indian men that also included truck farming in New Jersey is significant. Like other men in Marshall's fiction, he courts individuation, seeking manhood defined through Western lenses. Since one measure of that achievement—economic viability—is denied him in Bournehills, he volunteers for physical labor in Florida, where he believes his wages will enable him to support his girlfriend and his child. When neither the job nor fatherhood succeeds in satisfactorily establishing Vere's male identity (the baby dies while he is in Florida), his plans to rebuild an automobile and win the island's annual Whitmonday race bespeak his continued search for identity in the schematism of gender, in which he has little say.

Vere fails to affirm his male identity by having a child, not only because the child dies but also because his girlfriend's definition of manliness excludes Vere, whom she calls a "small, poor-behind country boy who don't have nothing to give but some baby every time you look around" (274). The young woman, like Vere, experiences the consequences of race, class, and gender. Although she is slightly characterized, the scene of confrontation between her and Vere is extremely revealing, especially when Vere becomes physically abusive and strikes her with a length of cane. "Her silence—but even more so her lean humped back, said she had long grown inured to such abuse, that she knew how to take it" (275). Her compliance with Vere's punishment ceases when he injures one of her dolls, "all dressed . . . in an exact copy of her lavish gown; and their spun-gold hair piled in the same elaborate tower of curls as her wig, was studded with fake jewels also" (272–73). This woman's identity is displaced and jeopardized because she perceives her race and class as undervalued by the dominant society. Her imitation of the dolls conveys her psychologically unhealthy rejection of self and most likely influences her rejection of the roles of mother or wife to Vere. Her response to Vere's damaging the doll "began at a high, with no build-up whatsoever; a sudden shrill atonal scream which rose and fell with the regularity of a siren . . . which called to mind, in its almost ritualistic fluting, the high-pitched, tremolant keening of Arab women mourning their dead (276). The mourning is for herself, but it might have foreshadowed Vere's death as well, since he literally kills himself through his effort to transform his image.

The automobile, symbolizing power, speed, and prestige, seems a predictable object with which a young man in search of an external representation of self might connect. It is important that Vere purchases a wreck of an old car—an Opel with a German motor and American body—to rebuild, making it over in his own image. Reconstructing the automobile is tantamount to his own rebirth: "It's got to be fire red, so when people see me coming they'll know for certain it's me" (242). The industrialized countries that dispossessed colonial subjects of their history, language, and culture also assassinated the male image. Thus, Vere's rebuilding of the automobile is destined to fail because he cannot re-vision himself through the tools of the West. Intuitively, his Aunt Leesy knows that he cannot succeed: to the messenger who brings news of Vere's death, she says, "It kill him, yes?" (368), rather than "Did the car crash?" or "How badly is he hurt?"

Vere's rebuilding of the Opel calls attention to himself, to an internal change that people attribute to the car: "It's the car make him feel he's a man," they said, even when they agreed with Leesy that the car "meant him no good" (347). It leads the annual Whitmonday race, as Vere had dreamed. He envisions himself celebrating with the other men, "although he had seldom before ventured into their midst, . . . he would join them today for a rum in the masculine intimacy of the shop" (364). On the last lap, however, the car begins to collapse: "It was as if the Opel, though only a machine, had possessed a mind, an intelligence, that for some reason had remained unalterably opposed to Vere, so that while doing his bidding and permitting him to think he was making it over into his own image, to express him, it had also at the same time been conspiring against him and waiting coolly for this moment to show its hand. . . . [Perhaps the collapse flowed] out of a profoundly self destructive impulse within the machine itself" (367).

Thus, Vere becomes a casualty in the pernicious fallout of the dynamics of race, gender, and class. His first effort at survival, the labor scheme in Florida, merely trades one thinly veiled form of economic exploitation for another. His second effort, a symbolic and unconscious effort to link his identity with the power of an automobile that he has rebuilt, illustrates a severe misperception of the forces arrayed against him and, by extension, against other workers in the Caribbean or in the United States. Marshall's vision involves systematically exposing multiple configurations of factors that impede spiritual wholeness. Her depictions of men of African descent reflect the research findings of sociologist Ronald L. Taylor, who writes that "the requirements of the male role turn male maturation into an achievement, an accomplishment purchased at considerable psychic cost" (147).

In Marshall's fiction, the worlds that men of African descent inhabit repeatedly place them at physical, emotional, and psychic risk. Deighton Boyce, the men of *Soul Clap Hands and Sing*, and Verson Walkes all illustrate fragmentation, emptiness, or hollowness. Even those like Mr. Challenor and Mr. Springer (*Brown Girl*) or Jerome Johnson (*Praisesong*), who are materially successful, prosper, but not without the sacrifice of wholeness. Beneath the displays of materialism lie fragmented beings whose misguided survivalist instincts become their legacy to their children or wives. Beryl Challenor, for example, is unable to distinguish her goals for the future from her father's goals for her. Clive Springer's rebellion against his parents springs from the same source—their rigidity in determining that his adult goals must replicate theirs. The depiction of these young people in *Brown Girl* indicates Marshall's perception of the liability of living in a society that exploits human beings. Selina's rebellion against the materialism of her mother and the victimization of her father propels her toward Barbados, the land of their origin. Although her journey back is not completed in Marshall's first novel, it is crucial in the author's exploration of spiritual wholeness, its barriers, and what may be required for its realization. What happens to the characters in both *Brown Girl* and *Soul Clap Hands and Sing* suggests that Marshall decided that women would be more receptive than men to the metaphorical journeys necessary to attain spiritual wholeness. Selina is, after all, poised for a significant stage of self-discovery, and women survive as the enlightened or renewed in *Soul Clap Hands*.

Through Merle Kinbona in *The Chosen Place*, Marshall explores the fragmentation endemic to the colonial experience. Against a Caribbean setting where the residual structures of colonialism are vividly rendered and where the dynamics of race, class, and gender are no less viable, Marshall locates temporary healing of a fractured self in the perception and use of language as a tradition within the black community. What is important in the delineation of Merle Kinbona is her intermediacy in Marshall's spiral toward spiritual wholeness. Through her, Marshall illustrates a fuller resolution of psychic fracturing, as if she were a middle-aged version of Selina Boyce.

"Talk" as Defensive Artifice: Merle Kinbona in *The Chosen Place, the Timeless People*

> [It] is not difference which immobolizes us, but silence.
>
> —Audre Lorde

In the culture of black people, verbal skill is highly prized and valued. Rapping, signifying, and the dozens, for example, are speech techniques used primarily to show verbal agility and wit, whereas storytelling, joke telling, and pulpit rhetoric function as modes of both entertainment and moral instruction.[9] Historically, talk has often been used to subvert or to overtly mystify communication with members of the majority culture; it has also functioned to protect the speaker, thus linking the ability to talk in certain culturally specified ways with maintaining physical well-being. In *The Chosen Place, the Timeless People*, Marshall draws upon this resource of the black community by creating a protagonist whose fragile mental equilibrium is sustained through the extravagance of her talk.

The replication of specific rhetorical tropes from the black community in a literary text acknowledges the connection between literary texts and cultural practices. Henry Louis Gates Jr.'s, argument for "signification [as] a theory of reading" (*Figures in Black*, 235) attests to the relationship between black artists and their community and to the multiple modes within African-American discourse that extend from the public functions of talk in black communities.[10] Recognizing the paradoxical, conscriptive, and protective qualities of black discourse, Marshall appropriates its public dimension to a private mode, thereby highlighting the black oral tradition and situating talk as integral to women's lives. Because discourse in black fiction includes examples of verbal agility and communication styles that are unique to blacks, it calls for attention to the public domain of its tradition even as it directs the reader toward the private spaces of the text.

George Steiner identifies a "strain of autism" in the language of poetry. "Language is focused on language," he writes, "as in a circle of mirrors" (164). Steiner's observation is applicable to fiction, as well:

for example, Toni Morrison's Milkman (*Song of Solomon*) assumes a reflective posture when he engages in a verbal duel with strangers in a rural store in Virginia. Milkman has grown up in a middle-class environment and never lived outside Michigan, and the Virginians have seldom (if ever) ranged outside of Shalimar. Nevertheless, these men, different in nearly every way, are identical in their ability to articulate the ritualistic insults that precede their fight. Milkman proves able in verbal sparring despite his difference in class. His ability to speak the language of the men of Shalimar argues for the existence of a common linguistic community across chasms of class differences and geographical boundaries.[11] Milkman and the Shalimar men recall Steiner's "circle of mirrors" as a consequence of both their enclosure (autism) and their reflection of cultural tradition. The performance-oriented discourse between Milkman and the Virginians is gender-specific and takes place in a public domain.

Black women's textual orality, although it similarly restructures the traditions of the black community, is more likely to occur within private spaces. Socialization and cultural tradition have historically relegated black women and their talk to private sanctums.[12] Although black women writers, for the most part, observe these private or interior spaces in their narratives, they explore the various uses of talk, for example, its self-healing properties and its ability to convey intimacy between black women. Barbara Smith believes that the "use of Black women's language and cultural experience in books *by* Black women *about* Black women [result] in a miraculously rich coalescing of form and content [that] takes their writing far beyond the confines of white/ male literary structures" (174). Women talk to each other the way they want to talk; within the embrace of their culture, they define and validate themselves through their talk. As they verbally assault the structures that continually demean them, they promote the healing of wounds carelessly inflicted by the outside world.[13]

The Chosen Place, the Timeless People offers a context for examining the relationship between literary text and cultural tradition because of the central function of the protagonist's discourse in the book. Marshall draws on the valued cultural art of talk to salvage Merle Kinbona's mental health. Merle uses talk to divert, subvert, and mystify, to conceal her self or to attack her enemies, and to mask her fragility and vulnerability. In short, talk becomes Merle's defense, and she is conscious of its effectiveness as a barrier against others' perceptions of her loss of psychological equilibrium. In a positive way, talk binds Merle's badly fractured self and sustains her. As important, talk becomes the means through which she initiates self-healing and potential wholeness.

The fragmentation that precipitates the necessity for Merle's talk originates in a history of public exploitation that ensnares her in a private way. As a West Indian woman, Merle's history, like that of U.S. blacks, increases the likelihood of her susceptibility to psychic fracturing.[14] For her, fracturing's disabling qualities—indirection, uncertain identity, and spiritual malaise—promote passivity and possible insanity. Merle's dysfunctional fragmentation, which is among the most extreme in Marshall's fiction, connects directly to Caribbean history more clearly than in Marshall's other texts. In *The Chosen Place*, character and place mirror each other; that is, a character's personal problems embody the troubled public history of the setting. People seldom exist independent of their culture or of their history, and Marshall's technique of bonding the public history of the setting with the private history of the characters illustrates this interdependency. Barbara Christian has characterized this phenomenon as "the delineation of personal characters . . . to show how individuals are distinctive features of the seemingly impersonal face of history. Time and timelessness and character and culture exist in a continual movement" (107).

Thus, the problems that precipitate Merle's fragmentation are of two kinds—personal and historical. As a black woman of inconsequential power, she reenacts the history of the island through her mixed birth (a white descended from a British forebear and black West Indian mother) and through an experience in London during college years (a power struggle between a wealthy white woman and Merle). The constant in these experiences is exploitation. Merle's personal history includes irreconcilable loss: her husband's desertion and the consequent loss of their baby girl. Merle's guilt about the woman and resultant self-deprecation, her inability to alter the events and regain her family, and her powerlessness in stopping the continuing exploitation of her community are the immediate sources of her psychological fragmentation.

As the main character who embodies the despoliation of the place, Merle controls the focus of *The Chosen Place*. Her personal loss and failure, in addition to her empathy with the islanders, the reality of her impotence, her anger, and the disparate strands of her identity, bring on significant long-term disability and spiritual malaise. The problems are enough to drive a woman crazy. In Merle's words, "You feel so helpless at times you want to scream like a mad woman or rush out and murder somebody. That's right" (228). Yet Merle neither commits murder nor goes mad.[15] Instead, Marshall depicts Merle's fragmentation symbolically—through her personal dress, the eclectic items in her bedroom, and, most strongly, the quality of her raging talk. Merle's physical appearance is evidence of more than questionable personal taste. Indeed, her attire embodies the conflicts of her multiple heritage of Africa, Europe, and the West Indies, as it reflects her interior disharmony. Each part expresses "a diversity and disunity within herself, and her attempt, unconscious probably, to reconcile these opposing parts, to make of them a whole" (5). Her dress, "cloth from the sun, from another cosmos, [might] have been found draped in offhand grace around a West African market woman. Pendant silver earrings carved in the form of those saints to be found on certain European churches adorned her ears. . . . Numerous bracelets . . . bound her wrists. . . . [Her face] might have been sculpted by some bold and liberal Bantu hand which had deliberately ignored all the other strains that had gone into making her" (4–5).

Merle's bedroom furnishings offer further evidence of her fragmentation: a bed from the estate of her British biological father; prints of planters' smiling wives and daughters, prints of dinner scenes picturing liveried slaves, and prints of black cane workers "filing in long columns up the ramps to the sugar mills with the canes on their backs bending them double" (400); and a drawing of a three-masted Bristol slaver, "rendered in cross section to show how the cargo, the men, women and children, the babies at breast, had been stowed away on the closely tiered decks" (401). Among her personal items are history books from her London school days, her dead mother's sewing machine, African print fabrics, dusting powder, and the "cruel iron-toothed comb she heat[s] to straighten her hair." These dissonant influences indicate the confusion of her identity. The objects in the bedroom symbolize the African slave trade, colonial intervention and exploitation, physical enslavement, assimilation of an alien culture, the erroneous public record of past events, and the prodigious personal effort needed to unify these components. While the eclectic dress and furnishings do not indicate only that Merle is unreconciled with her African heritage, they certainly do suggest that she has not embraced any single component of her cultural heritages. It is remarkable that Merle has resisted permanent peace through her comatose states and that she is able to maintain a perilous mental cohesion through talk, which prevents her irreconciled identity, the absence of her husband and daughter, and her despair in the presence of residual colonialism from driving her mad. She and her friends are aware that her grip is tenuous. When her precarious equilibrium is upset, for example, she enters a comatose state characterized by silence and dissociation. In Bournehills terms, " 'the head's out,' meaning Merle had sunk into one of her long, frightening, cataleptic states during which she was more dead than alive" (398). She flees "completely the surface of herself for someplace deep within where nothing [can] penetrate, leaving behind a numb spent face, a body which look[s] as if it had been thrown like a rag doll, its limbs all awry, on the bed and left there, and the dead eyes" (399).

Merle's ability to maintain the fragile balance between sanity and insanity through talk enables her psychological salvation. Otherwise, her fate would match that of Pecola Breedlove, Hagar, or Eva Medina.[16] Merle equates her talk with her identity: "I'm a talker. Some people act, some think, some feel, but I talk, and if I was to ever stop that'd be the end of me. And worse, I say whatever comes to my mind and the devil with it" (65). Her incessant speech assumes qualities of a "reckless" desperation, a "voice in race against both time and itself" (173), and "scarcely suppressed hysteria" (67). Rarely is there a moment for her listener to respond. The talk alone sustains her and maintains the imperative balance. Both the loudness of voice and the compulsive talk indicate that Merle "has not learned how to live with her bitterness and pain, how to control and disguise her rage" (90). The talk is a "camouflage and a shield" (229), like her smile, an insubstantial means of deflecting other people's perceptions of her fractured psyche.

Because a part of Merle's fragmentation may be attributed to her recognition of active colonialism, her talk often becomes a calculated public weapon with which she flogs individuals and a world that thinks reductively of the Bournehills residents. Loud talking ("hostile, aggressive speech that violates social convention [and] is assumed to be deliberate and with malice aforethought," Mitchell-Kernan, 330) substitutes, temporarily, for the power that her race and gender deny. Merle's style of talk and its purpose in certain instances are underscored by Michele Russell's belief that "when black women 'speak,' 'give a reading,' or 'sound' a situation, a whole history of using language as a weapon is invoked," that their "vocalizing is directly linked to a willingness to meet hostilities head-on and persevere" (25). An example of Merle's most caustic and vitriolic discourse occurs in a discussion about Bournehills' economics and politics. Responding to a plan that would entice tourist hotels to locate on the island but would also disadvantage the farmers, Merle articulately and succinctly defines one problem of economic stasis:

> 'Signed, sealed and delivered,' I say. 'The whole place. Is that what we threw out the white pack who ruled us for years and put you chaps in office for? For you to give away the island? For you to literally pay people to come and make money off us? Fifteen years without having to pay a penny in taxes! . . . Is that all that's possible for us in these small islands? Is that the only way we can exist? Well, if so, it's no different now than when they were around here selling us for thirty pounds sterling. Not really. Not when you look deep. . . . The chains are still on. . . . Haven't you fellows . . . learned anything from all that's gone on in this island over the past four hundred years? Read your history man!' (210)

Merle's loud talking, hostility, and malice are accepted by the Bournehills listeners without criticism or reciprocal hostility against her, however, because they understand it as her form of resistance and survival.

Merle's most sustained outburst in the narrative occurs, appropriately, in the sugar-processing factory called Cane Vale, the most visible symbol of industrial power and colonial oppression. Her practice of speaking passionately in public crosses the boundaries of setting in speech-performance expectations for men and women. In addition to loud talking, her talk encompasses the three kinds of speech behavior identified by Roger Abrahams's research in the Caribbean: talking sweet (identified not so much with the Euro-American world as with peasant household values); talking broad (rudeness, which is not always judged as bad behavior); and talking bad (identified with male life away from home) ("Training of the Man of Words," 118). Merle's invective against the tourist industry, for example, involves elements of both talking broad and talking bad, while it violates the good behavior associated with "talking sweet" and transcends the concerns of peasant household values.

Although protest speeches are not among the phenomena that Abrahams identifies, the publicly witnessed verbal fury that Merle unleashes against the Cane Vale supervisor almost certainly would be an occasion requiring a "man of words" of proven ability as the speaker ("Training of the Man of Words," 119). That Merle's verbal attack against the power structure is delivered in interior space does not lessen the exterior or public dimension of its impact. Traditionally and culturally, men have undertaken speech acts motivated by concern for the common welfare or interpreted as having public character. In Zora Neale Hurston's *Their Eyes Were Watching God*, for example, Jody Starks swiftly silences Janie before she can speak during public festivities: "Mah wife don't know nothin' 'bout no speech-makin'. Ah never married her for nothin lak dat. She's uh woman and her place is in de home" (69). And in *The Chosen Place*, women other than Merle are silent in the public arena. None of the women rages publicly at the closing of the cane-processing plant or argues about programs benefiting tourism and hurting farmers. This public dimension of Merle's talk, then, situates her in contradiction to the expectations of gender.

Not only does public speech distinguish Merle, but the content of her discourse also challenges sociolinguistic research. According to Cheris Kramarae, both black and white women's talk is characterized by "playing dumb, dissembling, and expressing frequent approval of others" (93), but because this statement fails to consider possible distinctions between women's social and economic classes and the styles and functions of their talk, it is suspect. It fails to engage the special functions of talk in African-American communities. Moreover, none of the qualities Kramarae identifies are ever apparent in Merle's discourse; instead they are indicated in the talk of a group of racially mixed, upper class, middle-aged women who spend an "entire evening inside alone, [apart from the men,] with little else to talk about except their children, the latest American fashions and their servants" (69). Interestingly, the black women in this group, except for Merle, are mostly wives of politicians and are therefore privileged socially and economically.

Merle's concerns—Bournehills' deteriorating economic situation and her personal inertia—find no release in frivolous conversation, although her incessant talk includes trivial details. In these instances the triviality acts only to offset the potential of insanity and is not an end in itself. Unlike the talk of the other women, Merle's discourse does not accommodate, concede, or pacify and is more likely to disrupt or anger than to provide light entertainment. Mae Gwendolyn Henderson believes that "the perspectives of race and gender, and their interrelationships, structure . . . discourse [to] account for racial difference within gender identity and gender difference within racial identity" (117). This process offers a credible means for differentiating Merle's discursive behavior from that of her women friends.

Paradoxically, although talk provides an essential means for Merle to release her frustration about public policy matters and improvement schemes, she remains silent about her private life, especially the loss of her husband and baby daughter. Retreating to Bournehills and embracing its problems allow her to submerge and camouflage the pain of personal loss and failure. Achieving the potential for wholeness, however, demands addressing all manifestations of her fractured psyche. Therefore, before Merle may initiate self-healing and restore her talk to agreeably normal levels, she must confront and reconcile her personal history and, in doing so, resolve the disruptive dichotomies of public and private.

Marshall not only situates talk as a resource for resistance in the African-American community but also centralizes it as a source of healing. Because Merle has used talk to bind her fragmentation, it is fitting that she also employ it as the primary means through which she reconciles herself. Through the intimacy of talk, Merle reveals her history to Saul Amron, her confidante and lover. His experience as a Jew and his loss and failure in his first marriage, in addition to his genuine caring for Merle and the Bournehills population, cement their friendship and enable Merle to tell him about her husband and daughter and the Englishwoman. She accepts personal responsibility for her artlessness in the relationship with the Englishwoman and for her deceit in the marriage. Permitting her talk to become revelatory rather than concealing initiates Merle's progression toward wholeness through self-healing. Through talk, she relinquishes her guilt for her role in losing her family and acknowledges her responsibility for the failure of her relationship with the Englishwoman.

Saul's wife, Harriet, a wealthy, socially elite woman, replicates the arrogance of the Englishwoman when Harriet also tries to bribe Merle. Harriet's behavior with Merle parallels the exercise of power and explicit control in colonizer-colonized relationships. Rejecting Harriet's money, Merle avoids obvious entrapment and manipulation. Her diatribe against Harriet, psychologically beneficial rather than enraging and destructive, significantly removes Merle from the role of victim and propels her towards recovering her lost dignity.

Although accepting personal responsibility for losing her family and exorcising the memory and influence of the Englishwoman are significant, Merle must also unify the disparate strands of her identity. Their reconciliation, essential in the total healing of her fractured psyche, depends on her continued personal control and assertiveness. Because Merle's cultural heritage and personal identity have been complicated by the relationships among her European, African, and West Indian components, the emergence of a dominant identity with which she is fully comfortable is essential. To that end, she alters her chaotic physical appearance to reflect a fresh interior sense of self. Her selling the silver earrings shaped like English saints (a gift from the Englishwoman) symbolizes the termination of that woman's mental custody of Merle, her rejection of European cultural domination, and the end of her guilt for her part in her own victimization. Using talcum powder to whiten her black skin and a comb to straighten her hair have inhibited her acceptance of the natural qualities of her African and West Indian heritages. Selling the items that symbolized her conflicting admixture of cultures suggests her liberation from a state of fragmentation. Cumulatively, these activities signal the end of Merle's debilitating passivity.

Because talk has offered salvation from insanity and has been a significant asset in the initiation of her self-healing, Merle recognizes (and verbalizes) that she has used it to camouflage her passivity and hold together her fractured self: " 'I'll never get around to doing anything with what's left of my life until I go and look for my child. . . . I'll just go on as I am,' she said. 'Doing nothing but sitting out on this veranda all day or down in that damp cave of a room feeling sorry for myself and blaming everyone and everything for the botch I've made of things. And talking. Oh, god, going on like some mad woman all the time but doing nothing. And letting the least little thing set my head out, but doing nothing' " (463–64).

At the conclusion of the novel, then, Merle is no longer immobile but has become active. Her effusive talk, replaced by normal conversation, will be productive, unlike the angry diatribes that "set her head out." As she travels to Africa in search of her daughter and husband and resurfaces from immersion in her problems and those of her community, the outlook for her wholeness of spirit is positive.

Talk has been essential to Merle's self-salvaging and healing. The excessive talk that has deflected, camouflaged, and shielded becomes muted after her reconciliation, for it no longer needs to be combative or hysterical or to race against itself and time. And if the prognosis for Merle's achievement of wholeness is good, then Bournehills, too, will someday be released from the stifling grip of its history. The island's regeneration, however, like Merle's, will need to originate internally and employ communal resources. The talk that enables Merle to bind her fractured spirit until she manages self-healing has existed within her community, where the "central impulse [of language] is survival and resistance" (Thelwell, 80). Marshall's use of talk in *The Chosen Place* invites the reconsideration of the bridges between cultural traditions in black communities and literary texts, for in this novel, talk serves as a significant means of cultural transference. Thus, the inherent relationship between a community resource and the initiation of a woman's self-healing invites a reading of *The Chosen Place* that engages a perspective that neither automatically nor artificially divorces the text from its origins in black culture. Approaching *The Chosen Place* from such a perspective immeasurably enriches the reader's perception of Merle as a woman ultimately reclaimed by the disregarded strengths of her community.

CHAPTER FOUR

The Journey Completed:
Spiritual Regeneration
in *Praisesong for the Widow*

If there is one thing African Americans and Native Americans
have retained of their African and ancient American heritage, it is
probably the belief that everything is inhabited by spirit. This
belief encourages knowledge perceived intuitively. —Alice Walker

Barriers to Regeneration

Before the publication of Paule Marshall's *Praisesong for the Widow*,
most black women's fiction neglected the subject of spiritual regeneration as a corrective means of transcending fracturing in the lives of their
troubled characters. Rather, the black female experience has primarily
been depicted through a lens of impediments, articulated relative to
the politics of race, class, and gender or juxtaposed with political, economic, and social problems. Deborah K. King is among the many femi-

nist researchers who have pointed out these "interactive oppressions" that circumscribe and provide a specific context for black womanhood (42).[1] Collectively, this fiction exposes a majority culture that represses, strangles, and diverts black women's attempts at meaningful participation in the nation's economic and political life. Calling attention to these oppressive measures and illustrating their spirit-deadening capability was a preoccupation in most black women's novels before the mid-1970s.[2]

Marshall's novels, however, have moved progressively toward spiritual regeneration. Even as early as *Brown Girl*, Selina's and Silla's experiences suggest that something greater than material, social, or educational success is essential for easing and satisfying the spirit: success as well as failure in these areas is achieved in that first book. But final resolution is unrealized in *Brown Girl*. The protagonist's decision to explore the dual spheres of her heritage leaves the novel open-ended.

It can be assumed that Selina will confront a historic past in the Caribbean that resonates with African retentions, but readers can only speculate about her reception of it. How will Selina respond to the vision of the islands that has driven Silla's memory and motivated her immersion in materialism? Like *Brown Girl*, *The Chosen Place* concludes with the anticipation of a journey, that of Merle Kinbona to Africa. But surviving a severely fractured psyche and undergoing "psychological reintegration" does not ensure that she will automatically experience spiritual renewal in Africa.[3] Although both Selina and Merle have survived fracture and stand poised for a journey rich with symbolic possibilities, this potential is not realized until *Praisesong*. In this novel, Marshall not only makes visible the abstract notion of spiritual wholeness but also develops its contiguous relationship to Afrocentricity. Thus, the paradigm relies on Marshall's Pan-African sensibility and centralizes the journey as metastructure.

Like both *Brown Girl* and *The Chosen Place*, *Praisesong* delineates significant barriers to spirituality, but *Praisesong* simultaneously emphasizes the complex process of spiritual regeneration. Writing about the obstructions in black women's lives as well as offering a way to transcend them situates Marshall uniquely in the black female literary tradition. She is consistent with her literary sisters in many ways, but her careful attention to a worldwide black community, much of which is spiritually bereft, significantly distinguishes her work.

Spiritual regeneration occurs within a strongly defined black cultural matrix. In *Praisesong*, the island of Carriacou, where the islanders have kept remnants of African culture, provides the setting for Avey's transformation. Some characters in other black women's novels—such as Pilate Dead in Toni Morrison's *Song of Solomon* and Mama Day in Gloria Naylor's novel of that name—demonstrate a state of spirituality without the process of achieving it having been instrumental to events of the text. In *Praisesong*, Marshall covers new ground as she posits the achievement of spirituality as the consequence of a regenerative enterprise of ritualistic and mythical scope. This uncommon occurrence and Marshall's progression toward it through *Brown Girl* and *The Chosen Place* require the exploration of how obstructions in the novels of other black women so engage protagonists' lives that spirituality is neglected in favor of survival.

The way that labor dominates the lives of black females forms an intriguing thematic connection among protagonists Lutie Johnson in Ann Petry's *The Street* (1940), Rosie Fleming in Kristin Hunter's *God Bless the Child* (1964), Mariah Upshure in Sarah Wright's *This Child's Gonna Live* (1959), and Silla Boyce in Marshall's *Brown Girl*. Each of these characters finds daily economic sustenance completely absorbing. Consequently, each works long and arduous hours outside the home, seeking, except in Rosie Fleming's case, to alleviate the brutal poverty in their children's lives. According to King,

> A black woman's survival depends on her ability to use all the economic, social, and cultural resources available to her from both the larger society and within her community. For example, black women historically have had to assume economically productive roles as well as retain domestic ones. . . . Labor . . . has been a distinctive characteristic of black women's social roles. It has earned us a small but significant degree of self-reliance and independence that has

promoted egalitarian relations with black men and active influence within the black family and community. *But it also has had costs.* (50, emphasis added)

Although the financial self-determination of these characters is an economic necessity, these texts dramatically illustrate the consequences of misdirected economic self-determinism. The protagonists become engrossed in the spiral of production and monetary reward. Without attention to African-American economic history, they view their labor in relation to the rhetoric of success in America. They implicitly accede to the ideal that sustained work and motivation will earn them success. They invest their selves in work in spite of institutionalized deterrents that preclude all but minimal or short-lived positive results. Their obsessive desire to succeed according to the values of the majority culture acts to distance them from the imperatives of their cultural heritage. Spiritual or literal death or despair is often the consequence.

Alienation in the socialist feminist sense of the term results because the burden of labor separates these women from a sense of meaning other than physical survival. The alienation inherent in the Newtonian worldview, specifically in its dissociation of the spiritual and material, addresses the distancing between cultural heritage and economic commodification. Women laborers sink to the level of a thing, a process Marx labels *Verdinglichkeit* (Donovan, 68–69). The specialization of labor for black women fundamentally alienates because it is always menial and many times disabling.

The work hours of Lutie Johnson in *The Street* are almost mild in comparison to Mariah Upshure's lifelong nightmare of relentless, nonlucrative, and backbreaking domestic and public work in *This Child's Gonna Live*. Easily among the most depressing books about a black woman's experience, *This Child's Gonna Live*, set during the depression near the Eastern Shore of Maryland, chronicles defeat for Mariah at every turn. The entire black community of Tangierneck is victimized by racism and economic inequity, but as a black female, Mariah is triply oppressed. Despite the grim and immediate problems of her life, Mariah fights defiantly for her children's survival. Although the novel depicts the pinnacle of motherly self-sacrifice, the disheartening premise of this work is that a black woman seldom overcomes institutionalized oppression, regardless of her spirit, energy, ethics, or love. Although it is not impossible for women lacerated by social structures to attain spirituality, the debilitating effect of physical labor effectively mutes other dimensions.

What sustains both Mariah Upshure and Lutie Johnson are their indomitable convictions that through superhuman labor they will amass sufficient capital to relocate their children from poverty and the ugly consequences it spawns. Both Wright's and Petry's narratives emphasize ineffectual labor that barely delays economic insolvency. Mariah's work includes shucking oysters (leaving home at three A.M. and walking seven miles in shoes lined with cardboard), digging potatoes, gathering greenery for wreaths, and working in a tomato cannery. Neither Mariah's labor nor her husband's attempts at sea farming and raising raspberries allows them to live in decent housing. At age twenty-three, Mariah already has three sons, her daughter has died four days after being born, and she is pregnant again. Poor health, substandard diet, and the devastating cycle of fruitless work and poverty, however, predict that this infant will die or endure the diseases that afflict the other children. (In fact, one of Mariah's sons dies of worm infestation.) The pathos in the title reflects Mariah's plea that the next child be born under conditions conducive to its survival.

Lutie Johnson is similarly trying to ensure the survival of her only son. Working while she attends business school at night to qualify for employment that supports an acceptable standard of living seems reasonable to Lutie: "All she had to do was plan each step and she could get wherever she wanted to go. A wave of self-confidence swept over her and she thought, I'm young and strong, there isn't anything I can't do" (44). Lutie's perception of self-empowerment quickly deflates, however, as Petry's narrative emphasizes the destructive forces that mean defeat for Lutie specifically and for African Americans generally. Lutie quickly comes to understand that her philosophy for getting ahead is blunted by a simple fact: she can neither earn enough money to do it nor triumph over her situation.

In *God Bless the Child,* however, Rosie Fleming believes that to triumph over her environment, she must merge, to some degree, with its seamy life. She observes that managers of the numbers racket earn money, so she enters that predominantly male domain as a collector of bets. The speed with which Rosie acquires money by working two jobs makes wealth dangerously important to her. Subsumed by its power, she manipulates the structures that perpetuate oppression. Unlike Lutie or Mariah, Rosie Fleming has no children to motivate her labor; rather, she hopes to buy a lavish house in the old white section of town where her grandmother had once been a domestic worker. Because of misplaced values inculcated by her grandmother, she wants to pamper her family and friends with expensive gifts. Rosie's three-job schedule produces physical deterioration and her outrageous spending brings financial disaster. "I want things," she says at one point. "I want things so bad I'd kill myself to get 'em" (65).

Working to purchase real estate connects *God Bless the Child* and *Brown Girl,* for that is Silla Boyce's motivation. Ownership of homes and businesses, a primary indicator of economic prosperity to the Barbadian immigrant community, becomes crucial to Silla. More than any other achievement, the title to the brownstone symbolizes an important step in economic assimilation that can be achieved through satisfying three goals: owning homes and businesses, acquiring rental property, and sending children to college as preparation for a profession. No sacrifice is too great for these goals; their realization justifies flight from the island homeland. This achievement also dilutes the venom of racial discrimination and soothes the pain of aching knees and backs for the women. In *Brown Girl,* the Bajan women take the initiative in house buying and often assume all financial responsibility. Silla's friend, Florrie, explains that the women were "doing it some of every kind of way. Some working morning, noon and night for this big war money. Some going to the loan shark out there on Fulton Street. Some hitting the number for good money. Some working strong-strong obeah. Some even picking fares" (74). Silla's pledge that she will sell her husband's island land to finance the purchase of the brownstone in New York testifies to the urgency of her motivation and joins her in spirit with Rosie.

The consequences of a materialist imbalance in black women's lives is significant in a discussion about spiritual death and spiritual regeneration. In *The Street,* Lutie Johnson releases murderous rage generally at the oppression of Harlem's 116th Street and specifically at Boots Smith, the small-time gangster who tries to procure her for his white boss. This act forces her to abandon her son to a reform school as she flees New York. Mariah Upshure, having accomplished none of her goals and having become mother to two more children because of a friend's death, tries to commit suicide. Rosie Fleming dies of physical exhaustion and lung complications, both exacerbated by her realization that the perfect world she envisioned and labored to attain is as flawed as her existence in a roach-infested apartment. Silla Boyce, like Rosie, purchases the brownstone but is left lonely in it. Silla's secondary goal is thwarted when her daughter, Selina, refuses to continue in college.

The Street, This Child's Gonna Live, God Bless the Child, and *Brown Girl* embody paradigms for economic success based on value systems antithetical to African-American spiritual survival. For black women, following this path results in spiritual death. Lutie Johnson compares herself to Benjamin Franklin, thinking that if he "could live on a little bit of money and could prosper, then so could she" (44). Similarly, she transfers the practices and values of the Chandlers, a wealthy white family for whom she had worked in domestic service, to her own life: "After a year of listening to their talk, she absorbed some of the same spirit. The belief that anybody could be rich if he wanted to and worked hard enough and figured it out carefully enough. [She and her young husband] hadn't tried hard enough, worked long enough, saved enough. There hadn't been any one thing they wanted above and beyond everything else. These people had wanted only one thing—more and more money—and so they got it" (32). But neither Benjamin Franklin nor the Chandlers encountered the politics of race or gender working negatively against them. Lutie forgets, as Majorie Pryse points out, that her sex and race "disqualify" her for achievement of that particular version of the American dream (117).

Similar value distortion misdirects Rosie's motivations in *God Bless the Child*. Trudier Harris has recognized the corrosive influence on Rosie of her maternal grandmother, Lourinda Baxter Huggs, who was also a domestic in a white, wealthy household. Harris accurately identifies Lourinda's faulty internalization of the materialistic values of her employers, which she accepts and inculcates in Rosie. The grandmother assumes the superior demeanor of her employers and values their palatial home and exorbitant luxuries. In contrast, Rosie's hairdresser mother tries to toughen her so that she might survive the environment that race, gender, and economic position will create for her.

Lourinda Huggs, called the "unsuspected antagonist" by Darwin Turner in his introduction to the novel, fails to note flaws in objects as well as in people; she judges only surfaces (xxi). Her devastating influence on her granddaughter leads Rosie also to value objects and people that are flawed and unworthy. Nevertheless, Rosie's perceptions are not entirely askew, for she refuses involvement with the community pimp, an ominous symbol of death. And though she is initially attracted to the gangster, Tucker, she finally marries the unassuming Larnie, a man who loves her for herself. In this regard, Rosie—like Lutie Johnson, Mariah Upshure, and Silla Boyce—is depicted as a character of considerable moral complexity. Lutie also refuses to compromise certain values that would guarantee a singing career and money. Mariah Upshure, forced to decide whether to assist the drowning Miss Bannie, whose survival would doom Mariah's father-in-law to violent death, rescues the woman.

Capitalist idealism infuses Silla Boyce's philosophy and her response to getting ahead in New York City. Her dream is no different from that of other West Indians or from the dreams of thousands of European immigrants who came to New York, the "capital city of the exile," between 1890 and 1920.[4] Her immigrant status differentiates her from the other characters discussed here and excuses a certain naivete because she, like Lutie, believes that her labor will eventually reward her.

Her response, shaped by economic deprivation and grueling childhood labor in the Caribbean, is to attune herself to the rhythms of capitalism. But it has no rhythms because capitalism lacks cultural specificity and therefore constitutes a sterile counterpart. Silla's synthesis is depicted through the metaphor of the machine. "I read someplace that this is the machine age and it's the god truth," she says. "You got to learn to run these machine to live" (103). Silla's philosophy of economic power and survival thus makes her compatible with the philosophy of the system and insures her economic survival but condemns her spiritual vitality.

Research on the psychological aspects of European cosmology on African Americans offers a cogent explanation of the materialist impulse and its damaging consequences. Joseph A. Baldwin's recognition of the influence of the Anglo-American community on non-Anglo communities sets out an oppositional dichotomy between Anglo-American and African-American cosmological schemata. His explanation reinforces the spiritual disintegration and emptiness of Mariah Upshure, Lutie Johnson, Rosie Fleming, and Silla Boyce and identifies the psychic damage that they experience. Anglo-Americans value "material reality, objects, things (i.e., physical characteristics, money, property, etc.) [that] denote one's value or worth, more often overriding personal character and human qualities" ("Psychological Aspects," 219).

When blacks accept majority-culture values, they perpetuate, "a survival thrust that is anti-Black, anti-Self and contradictory to their survival. . . . The process of cultural/psychological oppressions among African-Americans results in a condition of psychopathology 'misorientation.' . . . The Black person so defined obviously holds an incorrect and contradictory, yet organized and apparently quite functional psychological orientation within the framework of European-American cosmology" (219–21).

Baldwin's research identifies the consequences of a preoccupation with materialism in these women's lives. When capitalism, with its emphasis on labor and production, is considered along with the idealism of the American dream and the harsh economic conditions of many black women's lives, their only responses are calculated to assure economic survival, which, as it turns out, is essentially antiself behavior. Lloyd W. Brown notes Marshall's concern with black women whose "roles have been defined by powerlessness." He concludes that she analyzes power from the perspective of "social and psychological phenomena which simultaneously affect racial and sexual roles, shape cultural traditions, and mould the individual psyche" (159).

Ancestral Roles in the Regenerative Enterprise

> Physical and psychic integrity represents a fundamental condition
> for aspiring to the rank of ancestor. . . . The ancestor in Africa is
> always and everywhere an 'organic' member of the community of
> the living.—Dominique Zahan

Black women as writers critique the valuation of material possessions above character and morality, but they also recognize deliberate designs that thwart or restrict economic prosperity for African Americans yet also make prosperity more appealing. Sarah Wright, Kristin Hunter, Ann Petry, and Paule Marshall all demystify the consequences of obsessive materialism by blatantly exposing it. Their protagonists undergo personal and familial loss, physical illness, personality alteration, and literal death, among other problems. In studying cultural differences between Euro-American and African cosmology, Joseph A. Baldwin and other black psychologists have found fundamental differences in the two groups' social realities that "ultimately reflect their different racial cultural histories and their distinct approaches to the maintenance of their survival" ("Psychological Aspects," 216). Fiction by black women illustrates the schism that occurs when blacks—particularly women—ignore the politics (and lessons) of race, class, and gender and blindly subscribe to the American dream, but only Marshall implicitly asks, how African Americans can remain culturally moored and psychologically whole while participating in economic enterprises that almost guarantee fragmentation.

Before answering that question in *Praisesong*, Marshall created characters who either avoided psychological fragmentation or overcame it:

the ancestors to whom she pays homage in "To Da-Duh, in Memoriam." Da-Duh appears, Marshall writes, in *Brown Girl, The Chosen Place*, "Reena," "British Guiana," and *Praisesong*: "She's an ancestor figure, symbolic for me of the long line of black women and men—African and New World—who made my being possible, and whose spirit I believe continues to animate my life and work. I wish to acknowledge and celebrate them. I am, in a word, an unabashed ancestor worshipper" (*Reena and Other Stories*, 95).

Similarly, Toni Morrison recognizes the prevalence of ancestors in black fiction and notes how they influence the outcome of a story:

> And these ancestors are not just parents, they are sort of time-
> less people whose relationships to the characters are benevolent,
> instructive, and protective, and they provide a certain kind of wis-
> dom. . . . What struck me in looking at some contemporary fiction
> was that whether the novel took place in the city or in the country,
> the presence or absence of that figure determined the success or the
> happiness of the character. It was the absence of an ancestor that was
> frightening, that was threatening, and it caused huge destruction
> and disarray in the work itself. ("Rootedness," 343)

One explanation for the high visibility of the ancestor in the fiction of black women suggests a vital link between art and reality. Several black female writers acknowledge women as both source and inspiration in writing, particularly mentioning the presence of the benevolent female ancestor as a conduit between the past and the present. Gayl Jones, for example, recognizes the connection between personal experiences and black women writers: "With many women writers, relationships within family, community, between men and women, and among women—from slave narratives by black women writers on—are treated as complex and significant relationships" (Tate, "Gayl Jones," 92). Maya Angelou speaks more specifically about the role of the ancestor in fiction as seer and model: "Image making is very important for every human being. It is especially important for black American women in that we are by being black, a minority in the United States, and by being female, the less powerful of the genders. . . . We need to see our mothers, aunts, our sisters and grandmothers." (Tate, "Maya Angelou," 2–3).

Margaret Walker preserved one of her female ancestors in *Jubilee;* Walker credits her grandmother with transmitting the slavery story through oral tradition.[5] Alice Childress relates a similar experience: "Events from the distant past, things which took place before I was born, have influence over the content, form, and commitment of my work. I am a descendant of a particular American slave, my great grandmother, Annie" (112).

Recognizing the strength of their ancestors is confirmation of such a presence in black women's fiction. This influence is not restricted to women's writing, of course, but ancestors are highly visible in that arena and are likely to be female. They bridge history, melding present strategies with those of the past as they assume responsibility for instructing new generations in survival techniques. This cultural role is a part of the heritage of West Africa, where the elderly are revered. The ancestral presence, visible in nonfiction as well as fiction, is thus heavily valued as a factor in cultural continuity. Ancestors function as mentors, sustaining the moorings of fragile spirits.

Where are the ancestors in *God Bless the Child, This Child's Gonna Live, The Street,* and *Brown Girl?* Their absence from these texts signals loss for the women involved.[6] In the three-generational household of *God Bless the Child,* Lourinda Huggs as misdirected ancestor fails in her role. Because she has distanced herself psychologically from black culture by embracing the majority culture—which sees her only as a servant—she cannot have any ameliorating effect on her granddaughter, Rosie. Similarly, no ancestor guides or rescues Mariah Upshure in *This Child's Gonna Live,* although the minor character Aunt Saro Jane does befriend her.[7] Significantly, Lutie Johnson in *The Street* laments her dead grandmother, the ancestor whose sagacity might have centered and sustained her: "Granny could have told her what to do is [sic] she had lived. She had never forgotten some of the things Granny had told her and the things she had told Pop. Mostly she had been right.

She used to sit in her rocking chair. Wrinkled. Wise. Rocking back and forth, taking in the rhythm of the rocker. Granny had even foreseen men like this Super" (52).

Lutie's grandmother certainly would have served a role like Aunt Cuny's. In Marshall's fiction, elderly women like the grandmother have the feel of rightness about them. They evoke memories of old black women and men whose quiet security, earned by the privilege of age, denies questioning. Miss Thompson in *Brown Girl*, for example, steadies the turbulence of Selina Boyce's life. A southern woman who migrated to Brooklyn, Miss Thompson carries both physical and psychological scars of a southern racist encounter. Her perspective helps Selina temper her ambivalence and resistance during Boyce family frictions. Unlike the Barbadians, Miss Thompson's economic progress is negligible in spite of jobs as hairdresser and maid. Her generous and caring nature, in fact, mark her as insufficiently callous and self-serving to do more than survive in a system that demands fierce competitiveness. Her mentoring of Selina is invaluable to the girl's growth. In *The Chosen Place*, the elderly, psychically whole Carrington, more a strong presence than a developed character, attends to Merle Kinbona when her precipitous balance is temporarily lost. Leesy, on the other hand, has powers of healing and future vision, although she cannot save her grand-nephew, Vere, from his destructive efforts to prove his manhood.

Marshall pays homage to her own Da-duh by making the ancestors in her novels essential to the lives of modern black women and by conflating African cultural beliefs with African-American women's reverence for their female ancestors. Just as her earlier novels may be read as prologues to the potential of spiritual regeneration that she illustrates in *Praisesong*, so may the elderly women in the earlier novels be interpreted as rehearsals for the ancestors in *Praisesong*.

Marshall's most elaborately characterized ancestors are *Praisesong*'s Aunt Cuney and Lebert Joseph—mythical, timeless, sage, androgynous, and futuristic visionaries. Aunt Cuney, though literally dead, forces Avey to confront her ravaged spirit. Joseph redirects Avey to the island of Carriacou, and through his intercession, Avey reconnects herself culturally. Through Joseph's physical appearance and role, Marshall fuses the mythic with the real in these ancestors. Joseph, the Legba figure, brings together the real and psychic world as well. He is "one of those old people who give the impression of having undergone a lifetime trial by fire which they somehow managed to turn to their own good in the end; using the fire to burn away everything in them that could possibly decay, everything mortal. So that what remains finally . . . hidden within, out of harm's way [is] the indestructable will: old people who have the essentials to go on forever" (161). This description applies to all of the ancestors in Marshall's work.

The infusion of myth in the narrative through the ancestors marks a distinctive feature of the text. Both Aunt Cuney and Joseph, whose knowledge transcends human bounds, are elevated beyond ordinary stature. For example, Aunt Cuney's grandmother tells her in a dream that the child will be a girl before Avey is born. Thus, Avey becomes linked through dream and ritual with Aunt Cuney, whose beliefs and practices continue the process through the story of the Ibos. The story deliberately sustains spiritual integration: Aunt Cuney heard it from her grandmother and passed it on to Avey. Avey retains the tale until young adulthood, but she does so without understanding its meaningful design.

The ritual with which the story is invested communicates its value. During the summers, Aunt Cuney and Avey enacted the ritual twice weekly. With a large field hat over her headscarf and braids and wearing two belts, one at the waist and the other "strapped low around [her] hips like the belt for a sword," Aunt Cuney is joined with her African foremothers. Her "straight, large-boned mass and height," wearing of brogans, and fast-paced walk mark her as androgynous (32). The preparation, the walk, and the story comprise the ritual:

It was here that they brought 'em. They taken 'em out of the boats right here where we's standing. . . . And the minute those Ibos was brought on shore they just stopped, my gran' said, and taken a look around. A good long look. Not saying a word. Just studying the place real good. . . . And they seen things that day you and me don't have the power to see. 'Cause those pure-born Africans was

peoples' my gran' said could see in more ways than one. . . . Well
they seen everything that was to happen 'round here that day. The
slavery time and the war my gran' always talked about, the 'man-
cipation and everything. . . . And when they got through sizing
up the place . . . they just turned, my gran' said, all of 'em . . . and
walked on back down to the edge of the river here. . . . And they
didn't bother getting back into the small boats drawed up here. . . .
They just kept walking right on out over the river. Iron on they
ankles and they wrists and fastened 'round they necks. . . . But
chains didn't stop those Ibos none. Neither iron. . . . And they was
singing by then. . . . My gran declared she just picked herself up
and took off after 'em. In her mind. Her body she always usta say
might be in Tatem but her mind, her mind was long gone with the
Ibos. (38–39)[8]

Aunt Cuney's narrative represents her paradigm for the survival of
Africans in the New World. Like most tales in the African-American
and Afro-Caribbean traditions of storytelling, Aunt Cuney's is not designed to amuse a visiting New York child but rather to teach any child
how to live in the world without being subsumed by it. Its lesson is
that Avey must maintain separation between her mind and her body. If
she cannot physically remove herself, then she must protect her mental state regardless of her physical location. The story is intended to be
inculcated in Avey's life and to be passed on. Avey initially repeats it
upon returning to New York and later passes it on to her husband (who
believes), but the pressures of marriage and children displace the memory of Aunt Cuney and the story, and Avey fails to share the ritual with
her children.

The theme implicit in the coda of the Ibo story and the depiction
of Aunt Cuney's rural community joins West African cultural production to its transplanted setting in America. The neighborhood through
which Aunt Cuney and Avey walk en route to Ibo Landing, for example,
offers evidence of translocated cultural arts in everyday life. The herbal
healing practices of one neighbor, the carving ability of another, and
the vegetable growing of a third suggest that these inhabitants of rural

South Carolina have not veered too far from indigenous West African practices. The elders perform the ring shout in a church, a movement linked to African dance forms.

Aunt Cuney's intrusive and disruptive reentry into Avey's comfortable life (although Aunt Cuney is dead) is intended to metaphorically reposition Avey along the path to Ibo Landing from which she has severely strayed. Avey is middle class, with the house, furnishings, clothes, and attitude to substantiate her social position. The sixty-four-year-old widow vigorously resists Aunt Cuney, whose purpose, undergirded by myth, is clear. As Avey's ancestor, she becomes the catalyst in resurrecting Avey's memories of the past. Rather literally, she awakens the sleeper and begins steering her toward the realization that middle-class status has deadened her spiritually. Appropriately, Aunt Cuney stands along the path to Ibo Landing in Avey's dream, symbolically summoning Avey to retrace her walk to the Landing and back to her formerly moored status. Her insistent beckoning initiates a series of events that eventually reawaken Avey to the value of her cultural past and to the importance of keeping the lessons of the elders alive. The ancestral interference precipitates dreams, flashbacks, and journeys that cumulatively bring Avey to realize her fractured psyche. More important, though, the ancestors direct Avey through a process of spiritual regeneration.

Introducing a dead female ancestor through dream and re-creating her function through recalled ritual cleverly invigorate the narrative and position Avey as the adversary in defense of the class position that she and her husband fought to attain. But because Aunt Cuney is dead, the process of Avey's regeneration demands a live ancestor for its completion. In many ways Lebert Joseph becomes Aunt Cuney's live counterpart. Like her, he is androgynous, spiritually attuned to his heritage, and gifted with superhuman knowledge. His penetrating look marks him "as someone who possessed ways of seeing that went beyond mere sight and ways of knowing that outstripped ordinary intelligence (*Li gain connaissance*) and thus had no need for words" (172). He becomes Avey's primary director in both her literal and spiritual journeys and as such is invested with mythic dimensions. Eugenia Collier points out his connection to the African deity Legba (312). The apparent vacillation of his age from time to time and a physical description that makes him either horribly decrepit or jubilantly vigorous underscore his status as a figure of myth. The strategic placing of ancestors in this narrative—Aunt Cuney in the South, arguably a second homeland for African Americans, and Joseph in Grenada in the Caribbean, where spiritual proximity to the African heritage has remained vibrant—emphasizes cultural connectedness between widely separated communities. Continuing Aunt Cuney's role, Joseph stresses knowing the place and people of one's origins and the necessity of reverence for the "old parents." This philosophy specifically connects Joseph to West African cultural beliefs, and it reinforces his role in reanchoring Avey to her proper cultural axis (Zahan, 49).

One compelling element of *Praisesong*'s narrative is its retrospective sequences. Aunt Cuney's powerful story of the Ibo walk is one such example. Joseph's solid balancing on an imaginary line separating the past and the present is another. Because Avey has lost the meanings that Aunt Cuney so carefully gave her, the process of regaining them necessarily involves a retrospective of her life and her losses. Her metaphorical journey back, aptly titled "Sleeper's Wake," becomes a reversive one, compelling her intimate self-examination and consequent redefinition.[9] Avey's journey is aptly described by Deborah McDowell's insight that although the black female journey may be social and political, it is essentially personal and psychological because the female protagonist is in a state of becoming ("New Directions," 195).

During her metaphorical journey, Avey's memory centers on the barriers to spiritual renewal that join her and her husband's economic efforts with those of Lutie Johnson, Rosie Fleming, and especially Silla Boyce. Unlike them, however, Avey's ancestor had given her the paradigm of the Ibos and she had been culturally moored as a young, married, working-class woman. She becomes unmoored almost in direct proportion to her economic rise. The example of Avey and Jerome makes a sensitive addition to depictions of psychic fragmentation as the consequence of environment and materialism. Marshall depicts their economic success in subtle contrast to their spiritual demise, which, significantly, includes their loss of individual and cultural identity. Jerome works two jobs and attends business school at night to earn a degree, an exhaustive schedule that requires twelve years of submerging anger and masking frustration. Conversely, he and Avey lose time for after-work dancing or reading poetry in their apartment.

Avey's memory of their married life in a fifth-floor walk-up apartment on Halsey Street is among Marshall's most discerning and realistic depictions. Halsey Street becomes a metaphor for hundreds of similar streets in hundreds of cities where economic deprivation dominates; where underfed, poorly clothed children live; and where hopelessness and defeat threaten to complete the ravaging of the black psyche. It is synonymous with 116th Street in Petry's *The Street*, with the narrows in Petry's novel of that title, with Brewster Place in Gloria Naylor's *The Women of Brewster Place*, with Fulton Street in Marshall's *Brown Girl*, and with All-Bright Court in Connie Porter's novel by that name. But Marshall's illustration of the street's force, of its creative strength in assaulting its inhabitants and injecting them with despair, is compressed into a single Tuesday-night argument between Jerome and Avey. Pressures of a third pregnancy, a young marriage, and unwarranted jealousy in a climate of poverty drive Avey to shout words that haunt them the remainder of their lives together: "Goddamn you, nigger, I'll take my babies and go!" (106). That argument and the couple's realization of the power of the street catapults Jerome into studying for a degree in accounting and into working multiple jobs for twelve years, during which time he and Avey "commit a kind of spiritual suicide" (Christian, *Black Women Novelists*, 77):

> He went about those years like a runner in the heat of a long and punishing marathon, his every muscle tensed and straining, his body being pushed to its limits; and on his face a clenched and dogged look that was to become almost his sole expression over the years. He ran as though he had on blinders to shut out anything around him that might prove distracting. . . . Even things that had

once been important to him, that he needed, such as the music, the old blues records that had restored him at the end of the day, found themselves abandoned on the sidelines, out of his line of vision. (*Praisesong*, 115)

Avey and Jerome succeed, finally, in the first of the journeys that mark their economic rise—moving from Halsey Street to a larger apartment and then to the house in North White Plains. After a year of being refused employment in large companies, Jerome canvassed neighborhood businesses, became their accountant, and opened his own office, which enabled the couple's economic success. But Avey wonders, "Would it have been possible to have . . . wrested, as they had done over all those years, the means needed to rescue them from Halsey Street and to see the children through, while preserving, safeguarding, treasuring those things that had come down to them over generations, which had defined them in a particular way. The most vivid, the most valuable part of themselves!" (139).

Avey's question is never articulated in *The Street, God Bless the Child, This Child's Gonna Live,* or *Brown Girl.* Petry, Hunter, and Wright offer valuable depictions of women working for economic solvency and, paradoxically, of their physical impairment in the process, but that they are spiritually bereft is implied rather than overtly addressed within the novel. It is significant that the question is asked in *Praisesong,* because posing it makes recognition of psychic damage explicit. And it is significant that black cultural expressions—jazz, blues, poetry, dance—are valued for their stabilizing qualities in the psychological space of one's home. Dance, in particular, plays a major role in Avatara's psychic reintegration, years after Halsey Street.

Quests, Rituals, and Transformative Spirituality

> Traditional festivals and art forms must not remain redundant celebrations of a dead past, but must be transformed to give sustenance to a living and changing present.—Abena P. B. Busia

> The effectiveness of rituals, however, lies in their contexts. Their utility as processes of demarcation inheres in their irreversibility. When a young person is read out of childhood or a woman is read into motherhood through prescribed rituals, neither can return to his or her preritual status.—Houston Baker

Avey's metaphorical odyssey from a fractured self to spiritual regeneration is buttressed by several literal voyages. An earlier trip from Halsey Street to suburban North White Plains signifies the "classical journey of the black family that moves from accepting the crumbs to eating a piece of the pie that is the offering of corporate America" (Pollard, 289). The ideology of this representation of the American dream causes Avey's subsequent travels of which her journey to Carriacou is among the most important, because it restores her to herself and to her community. The extensive criss-crossing of literal and metaphorical journeys in *Praisesong* comprises a metastructure within the narrative. Her travels intertwine with dream, symbol, and ritual to establish motifs of circularity characterized by progress and completion. Avey's journeys signify the physical and cultural displacement of the African diaspora.

It is therefore appropriate that journeys inform this text as well as Avatara's experiences, for their presence reinforces her individual experience within the collective destiny. Avey's childhood journeys from the North to the South (from New York to the sea island of Tatem, South Carolina) reverse the great migration of southerners to northern cities in the pre–World War I years. In South Carolina, the walks to Ibo Landing and the story of the Ibos walking across the water back to their homeland encodes the crucial lesson of maintaining distance between body and mind to ensure African-American psychic survival in a hostile culture. Keith A. Sandiford astutely assesses the importance of the landing both literally and metaphorically, seeing it as a site where "embattled forces of myth and history struggle for hegemony" and identifying Aunt Cuney's visits as "an anti-historical gesture" (374, 377). Aunt Cuney tells the story to the child Avey and thus passes on the tradition of the griot. Through her specific preparation for and journey to the landing, Aunt Cuney teaches the centrality of ritual. Avey's aborted ocean cruise, an exercise in middle-class leisure and luxury, places her in Grenada. The voyage from Grenada to Carriacou by schooner re-creates the fear, misery, and horror of the Middle Passage experienced by her African ancestors.

Avey's journeys, particularly after fleeing the ship to travel to Grenada and Carriacou, constitute a quest motif. Marshall's extensive merging of reality and ritual and stabilization of the narrative in African cultural retentions in the Caribbean becomes the novel's coup. The quest motif, characterized by individual transformation and community reentry, invites the analysis of Avey's experiences from the perspective of traditional quest narratives, although Marshall's protagonist is a sixty-four-year-old black widow rather than the traditional young Euro-American male. Marshall notably portrays this traditional spiritual quest as one that agrees with and reflects African-American and Afro-Caribbean cultural experiences.

Avey Johnson's behavior complies with Joseph Campbell's explanation of the spiritual quest, involving "departure, fulfillment, [and] return" (136), in which protagonists experience "the supernormal range of human spiritual life and then [return] with a message" (123). They leave the present world and travel until reaching "what was missing in [their] consciousness in the world [they] formerly inhabited" (129). The moral objective is to preserve a people (127). Avey's rash departure from the cruise liner, the act that initiates her quest, follows unexplained dissatisfaction, distorted visions, and strange dreams. Her attempt to return to the familiar surroundings of her home in North White Plains is thwarted. Her retrospective and evaluative journey through the stages of her life and her realization of necessary change (in an aptly titled section, "Sleeper's Wake") are part of the protagonist's experience. Lebert

Joseph and Aunt Cuney propel Avey toward the events that will renew her acknowledgment of confraternity with the world black community.

Joseph is necessary not only because the elderly Aunt Cuney could not logically remain alive when Avey is sixty-four years old (unlike Milkman's enabling rescuer, Circe, in Toni Morrison's *Song of Solomon*), but also because both he and Aunt Cuney connect African-American, Afro-Caribbean, and African culture retentions. The ancestors represent a generation reliant on the oral culture and more conversant with cultural behaviors and practices linked with West Africa. Under their influence, the symbolic internal purging of the blockage that has obscured Avey's communal identification occurs. Significantly, it occurs on board the schooner en route to Carriacou, and the fete in honor of the ancestors.

Although the journey to Carriacou bonds Avey with her African progenitors during their severance from their homeland, it also encompasses much more. A sermon that she recalls from her childhood has a specific function: like preachers in the works of Zora Neale Hurston and James Weldon Johnson, the minister in Avey's memory delivers the story of Christ's resurrection in the tradition of the African-American pulpit orator whose style transforms the King James version into the idioms and nuances of black English. His "strangled scream, stolen from some blues singer" (199) further joins his performance to the folk of his audience, as their response to his call links them all to a West African cultural behavior. As Avey recalls the preacher's demand that the congregation rid themselves of "stones of sin," Avey rids herself of the spiritually strangling materialistic force symbolized through food images, the bloated mass that has marked her extravagance. The sermon, the women on board the schooner (who remind her of church-women from her childhood), and the murmured "bon" chorus from the schooner passengers (resonating with the response of the congregation) conflate Christianity, the Middle Passage, West African cultural behaviors, and the transit of African peoples. Avey's loss of control over bodily functions signifies continuation of her return to a childlike state, a process that began during her recollection of life on Halsey Street and an essential state that precedes completion of the journey.

Although she lies alone in the darkened deckhouse where the women lead her, she feels the presence of other bodies crowded with hers: "A multitude it felt lay packed around her in the filth and stench of themselves, just as she was. . . . Their suffering—the depth of it, the weight of it in the cramped space—made hers of no consequence" (209).

This experience on board the schooner revives the Middle Passage, the most crucial journey in the history of black people; moreover, it reinforces and enhances the prominent theme of cultural interconnectedness by merging Avey's psychic horror with the experience of her African ancestors. This is Avey's "journey back" (to echo Houston Baker), her near return to the source for spiritual reclamation. The connections among people of the African diaspora that Marshall symbolically and literally illustrates are instrumental to this text. Thus, the slender threads that Avey remembers extending "from her navel and from the place where her heart was to enter those around her" and make her "the center of a huge wide confraternity" serve as metaphorical connections among people who share a cultural origin (190–91).

Another step in Avey's progression toward spiritual reintegration, the literal cleansing of her body, is performed by Lebert Joseph's daughter, Rosalie Parvay. After bathing Avey's body systematically and ceremoniously, she oils and massages it. Parvay's formality of touch defuses its physical nature. Marshall retains the sensual quality of the massage of Avey's thighs, however, deliberately connecting their invigoration to Jay's manly joy. When Rosalie's hands reach the upper half of Avey's legs, she works the "sluggish flesh as if it were the dough of the bread . . . [until] the warmth, the stinging sensation that was both pleasure and pain passed up through the emptiness at her center. Until finally they reached her heart" (224).

The laying on of hands reflects a cultural tradition of black women. Joanne V. Gabbin recognizes such contact as a symbolic act of blessing, healing, and ordination . . . that bestow[s] some gift" (247). This practice, particularly evident in the recent fiction of black women as a tactic for reclaiming the spiritual dimension of a character, appears, for example, in Naylor's *The Women of Brewster Place*, where Mattie's persistent bathing and massaging of Ciel summons her back from literal and spiritual demise during the traumatic afterm?th of Ciel's child's death. Laying on of hands is featured, too, though in more complexity, in the redemption of Velma Henry in Toni Cade Bambara's *The Salt Eaters*. The physical revitalization of Avey's moribund flesh is an essential prerequisite to her readiness for spiritual wholeness. It is an act that also symbolically reconnects her with women's mystical capabilities.

The ceremony in Carriacou brings together spiritual, literal, and social links between black West Indians and their African ancestors. Avey's presence joins blacks from the United States with their West Indian brothers and sisters. Marshall has foreshadowed this most important connection several times in the novel. The elderly West Indian women on board the schooner might have been "the presiding mothers of Mount Olivet Baptist church (her own mother's church long ago)" (194). The crowd of islanders awaiting voyage, their "bodies, the colors and sounds, the pageantry of the umbrellas were like frames from a home movie she remembered Marion had made on her last trip to Ghana." Marian's film narrative had included mention of a "New Yam, of a golden stool that descended from the sky, and of ancestors who were to be fed" (187–88).

Avey's various journeys and Lebert Joseph's machinations have created this vital connective point where the festivities in memory of the elders are performed. Avey's walk on Carriacou transports her through darkness to a small clearing on a hillside, a "large denuded dirt yard" where the ceremony for the ancestors takes place (234). In African belief systems, earth anchors humankind, predominating in African myths, stories, and legends (Zahan, 22–24).[10] Therefore, the climax of Avey's regenerative enterprise occurs in its proper setting, for the activities performed on this bare earth restore her cultural properties. The ceremony—a curious blend of half-remembered names and West African practices such as the libation to appease the ancestors, the call-and-response songs to honor family names, and the circular dance accompanied by rum keg drums (replicas of African drums)—reaffirms the participants' honoring, retention, and transmission of their cultural origins. The ceremony is a reminder, as well, of cultural practices lost in the maelstrom of history: The drummer's "single, dark, plangent note . . . like that from the deep bowing of a cello, sounded like the deep distillation of a thousand sorrow songs. . . . The theme of separation and loss the note embodied . . . summed up feelings that were beyond words, feelings and a host of subliminal memories that over the years had proven more durable and trustworthy than the history with its trauma and pain out of which they had come" (244–45).

Marshall's choice of Carriacou as the site of Avatara's spiritual reintegration is not capricious, for its isolation, particular history, and cultural and social homogeneity, distinguish it from other societies in the British West Indies. When Marshall visited the island in the 1960s she discovered its retention of a "full fledged ancestor cult," and the "Big Drum or Nation Dance . . . [as] still the representative ritual form" (Michael G. Smith, 9–10). In the 1950s nearly all of the island's population was of African descent because an economic breakdown of sugar cultivation had dissipated the planter class. The reduction of ethnic complexity meant that Carriacou developed its own society and culture freed of the influence of creole elites (Michael G. Smith, 33–35). In the Carriacou Big Drum, songs and dances "are attributed to the African 'nations,' or tribes, from which the slave population of Carriacou was drawn, [and] are combined with secular songs and a cult of ancestor-worship. Big Drum songs are differentiated by their tribal origin such as Ibo, Moko, Congo, Temne, Mandinka, Chamba, Kromanti (Akan), and it is probable that these were the principal groups from which the Carriacou slaves came. The secular dances of the Big Drum in Carriacou—Kalenda, Juba, Belair, Granbelair, Banda, etc.—are differentiated by rhythm and dance form" (Michael G. Smith, 10).

The ancestor cult exists alongside Christianity on the island: "Our old parents believe in God faithfully; *and the Word of God is the word of our old parents*," an islander states in Michael G. Smith's study (139). Carriacou residents believe that communication with ancestors comes through dreams, and they give solemn reverence to each occurrence. If ancestors' requests are not granted, punishment follows. Women are message receivers, and elderly women receive personal messages as well as those for the community (Michael G. Smith, 140–42). Thus, Aunt Cuney's and Lebert Joseph's presence and power, the dream that dislodges Avey from the cruise, and her transformation through the intercession of her ancestor—all foregrounded in West African ancestral cults—have a basis in African cosmological systems.

Avey's participation in the circular dance of ancestral reverence therefore resounds with connective significance both for her personally and for the meaning of the novel. In the circle, a geometric formation that signifies continuity, black West Indians and black Americans symbolically join black Africans. Dance and music as cultural relics fit this ceremony of cultural reconciliation because of their centrality in the lives of African peoples. Africans are "born, named, initiated into manhood, warriored, armed, housed, betrothed, wedded and buried to music," which pervades all ceremonies, sustains community life, expresses group identity and solidarity, and serves to express or record the "dynasties, migrations, hardships and sufferings, defeats and victories" of the people (Kwabena Nketia, 151–54). Similarly, Frantz Fanon sees dance in the colonial world as the place where "the most acute aggressivity and the most impelling violence are canalized, transformed, and conjured away. The circle of the dance is a permissive circle: it protects and permits. . . . [It reflects] the huge effort of a community to exorcise itself, to liberate itself, to explain itself" (45). Marshall views "dance as ritual celebration, as renewal, as perhaps the most profound expression of the confraternity" of people of the African diaspora (Marshall, lecture).

Dancing the Carriacou Tramp comes naturally to Avey. She had performed it before, standing with her great-aunt on the dark road in Tatem, South Carolina, across from the church imitating "the old folk shuffling in a loose ring inside the church" (248). Her ease in performing the step signifies the retention of African practices in southern culture. The ceremony, as Barbara Christian has recognized, ritualistically joins several black societies: "the Ring Dances of Tatem, the Bojangles of New York, the voodoo drums of Haiti, and the rhythms of the various African peoples brought to the new world" ("Ritualistic Process," 157). More specifically, Sterling Stuckey's research illustrates that the ring shout was pervasive during slavery in the United States, transcending the differences of various African ethnic groups and unifying them. It functioned ceremonially in honoring the ancestors and in the burial ceremony (11–12). Numerous oral accounts by former slaves in the Georgia Writers' Project–Works Progress Administration's *Drums and Shadows* recall the measured solemnity of the drum and the circle dance at funerals (66, 143, 180, 184).

Lebert Joseph's temporary stoppage of the moving circle after observing Avey and his "profound, solemn bow that was like a genuflection" (250) acknowledge Avey's rebirth. Her materialistic excess and psychic dislocation are dead, and her disavowal of her mission as a griot in the tradition of her great-aunt is at an end. In a ceremony to honor ancestors, Avey is an initiate. In a ceremony that Africans in America retained to acknowledge their dead (who were buried at night, according to *Drums and Shadows*), Avey's cultural unmooring is dead. She is reborn, then, as a griot, an ancestor, a woman confirmed in her displaced African culture. It is therefore compelling that Avey reclaim her given name, Avatara, chosen by her great-aunt and sent before she was born. The *Oxford English Dictionary* defines *Avatara* as the descent of a deity to the earth in an incarnate form, certainly a meaning consonant with Avatara's presence and the ancestor's role in the text.[11]

The remaining task in Avatara's spiritual quest, her community reentry, is problematic for some critics. Missy Dehn Kubitschek, in particular, compares Janie Crawford's community reentry in *Their Eyes Were Watching God* with that of Avatara based on Janie's "self-relevation and friendship for Pheoby." Janie's story positions her personal experience against the background of her mother's and grandmother's histories. Avatara, however, will "communicate tribal myth rather than her own life," retelling the Ibo story as Aunt Cuney had done. Kubitschek believes that this method will only re-create the "same exact experience for her grandsons that [Avey] had with her great-aunt" (88). Kubitschek's dismissive reading of Avatara's experiences ignores several quantities. The inference is not that Avatara's story will exclude her personal odyssey, for she will begin with the Grenadian cab driver: "She would tell him . . . about the living room floor in Halsey Street . . . [about putting] on the records after coming in from work, [when] she had felt centered and sustained" (254). The logical implication is that she will also include the post–Halsey Street years; Jay's economic ascendency, when they both became unmoored; and those details of her personal experiences that demonstrate the consequences of capitalist intrusion to the detriment of spiritual preservation. The tribal myth, which contains the substance for spiritual salvation, encodes the means for avoiding Avey's experience. It is therefore unreasonable to assume that Avatara's narrative will reinscribe her alienation on others. Neither the griot nor her message is "invariant," as Dubitschek claims, but it is a cautionary tale, celebratory in its emphasis and conclusion.

Karla Holloway's position that the end of *Praisesong* "merely contains a promise of wholeness" (119) more reasonably questions the outcome of Avatara's community reentry, for the text concludes with her preventive strategy but not its actual implementation. Nevertheless, because Avatara's encounters have bound up her fragmented psyche, spiritual restoration has occurred, and her strategy for saving others confirms her generosity. These qualities bespeak not a promise but rather a condition of spiritual wholeness that makes possible her immersion in the preservation of her cultural community. This is a primary function for a psychically integrated person.

Having acquired vision and spiritual solidarity, Avatara Johnson will return as a recovered self, and the community will benefit. She will seek to prevent or to curb the psychological distancing of young blacks from their communities, to impart to them Aunt Cuney's concept of maintaining proper distance between body and mind as the means by which they might avoid the materialistic morass of American society, which is antithetical to their African properties. She will begin with her family and enlist the help of her daughter, Marion, in "spread[ing] the word" (255). She will reopen the house on the sea islands during the summer, summon her grandchildren there, and repeat the Ibo Landing ritual. At home in New York she will rescue others as well: "Her territory would be the street corners and front lawns in their small section of North White Plains. And the shopping mall and train station. As well the canyon streets and office buildings of Manhattan. She would haunt the entranceways of the skyscrapers. And whenever she spotted one of them amid the crowd, those young, bright, fiercely articulate token few . . . she would stop them" (255).

As a character who has completed the mythical and psychological quest, Avatara might be compared to Milkman Dead in *Song of Solomon* rather than to Janie Crawford: Avatara, like Milkman, has undergone self-transformation by traveling through myth.[12] Avatara will return to Tatem, South Carolina, where she will reinstate the walk to the landing, retell the myth about the Ibos, and teach the cautionary distance between mind and body. Spiritual rebirth has empowered her to perpetuate tradition and, perhaps, will invest her with the foresight to reclaim the spiritually bereft.

But what of Milkman? He returns to Michigan to his community only to be knocked senseless and hog-tied by Pilate in retaliation for Hagar's madness and death. He is not rewarded at the end of *Song of Solomon*. Rather, he is seen positively in an image of liberation or ambivalently in a posture of escape. Both Avatara and Milkman have been spiritually renewed, but only she will benefit the community. It is therefore tenable to say that while black men's culture orients itself toward individual objectives, the outcome of Avatara's spiritual rebirth reinforces black women's culture by investing them with the priorities of the community and its survival. Avatara's planned activities, in fact, strongly suggest that she has satisfactorily reclaimed spirituality and that her new role as ancestor is inseparable from considerations of community. According to Dominique Zahan, community connections constitute a "fundamental condition for aspiring to the rank of ancestor. . . . The ancestor in Africa is always and everywhere an 'organic' member of the community of the living" (49–50). Thus, Avatara's position at the novel's conclusion is consistent with ancestor requirements in African philosophy and with the protagonist's successful completion of quest in Campbell's study.

Avatara's quest and return to the community thus fulfill the potential began in *Brown Girl*. Her cautionary tale offers one way to survive in a capitalist society that oppresses and deprives. It is a crucial lesson that acknowledges genetic memory in re-creating cultural connections that have been severed. Marshall has written this story with discrimination and love because she knows it encodes a lesson vital for all descendants of Africans who survived the Middle Passage.

Daughters: Some Consequences of Journeying

The generations of white folks are just people but the generations
of colored folks are families.—Lucille Clifton

Daughters. Sons. Mothers. Fathers. Wives. Husbands. Each word signifies a relationship, an intimate and personal connection between human beings that often touches the depths and heights of emotion and passion. Being referred to as a daughter, son, mother, or father of the community is usually endearing and honorific, because the implication is that the community, like the family, has been instrumental in nurturing and defining someone whose success reflects admirably on the group. Paule Marshall's *Daughters* illustrates how sons and daughters give back to a community when it has effectively shaped its members. On the other hand, if a community has been dispossessed by colonialism, then its ability to shape its members has been impaired.

Daughters is charged by a chorus of men and women in various relationships with their communities and in different stages of self-definition. Unlike *Praisesong,* this novel does not focus on the protagonist's movement toward spiritual wholeness. Rather, Marshall initially centers reader attention on a constellation of characters, primarily women, before she focuses on a mother and daughter and then more narrowly on the daughter, Ursa MacKenzie. The central conflict involves Ursa, a young woman whose mother and community have provided sufficient culturally stabilizing experiences for her psychic wholeness. This character illustrates attributes of spiritual wholeness early in the narrative, qualities that she calls forth to enable her political and personal liberation from a domineering father.

Daughters is significant for its depiction of how spiritually whole women can comport themselves in both private and public spheres. The characteristics of Ursa and other psychically integrated women—Ursa's friend, Vincreta "Viney" Daniels, and Ursa's mother, Estelle—illustrate Marshall's concept of journeying beyond spiritual wholeness to find congruences between the personal and the political. If characters in *Daughters* are collapsing the distance between the personal and community concerns, then it follows that they have roundly emerged from "confine[ment] to private spaces [and] largely excluded . . . from the historical events that obsess and overdetermine the men's lives and experiences" (Gikandi, 197). This statement, perhaps applicable to many emergent women, does not fit many psychically integrated women.[1] It is valid, unfortunately, for many women who are still relegated to a secondary tier of existence or whose experiences are solely confined to home and family production.

One significant consequence of spiritual wholeness, *Daughters* suggests, is a vision that resists self-absorption to embrace collective definition. Although gender, race, and class proscriptions continue to affect the lives of most women in *Daughters*, spiritually whole women envision and work for sociopolitical and economic improvement for their communities. Marshall's multivocal text, which allows the unfolding narrative to emerge through numerous character perspectives, also permits a comparative assessment of the experiences of numerous women.[2]

Among the daughters of Triunion, Astral Forde, Malvern, and Celestine Marie-Claire Bellegarde comprise three different gendered experiences and three examples of self-definition. Their Third World lives suggest that, given similar social and economic origins, it is impossible to identify a homogeneous experience. At best, each woman merely symbolizes a group of women. Malvern and Astral function as narrative foils for each other. The differences in their economic and social lives are predicated not on chance or educational opportunity but on Astral's "prized hair and creamy skin, the straight white people features" (176). Thus, the value accorded to skin tone and hair texture, a phenomenon historically rooted in slavery, continues to influence economic and social standing. This inheritance encodes a victimization of women structured by insistent productions of history, race, and class.

Astral, living out the definition of her name, which means belonging to the stars, experiences consistent ascension in work and class, while her friend, Malvern, experiences the deterioration of an already poor economic and social situation. Astral's improved class status points up the connection between gender and economics, since her rise is predicated on both her physical appearance and an unarticulated understanding that, in exchange for sexual favors, men of economic and social standing (including Primus Mackenzie, an educated island politician) will assist her job preparation by paying for courses or hiring her. The intercession of various men thus facilitates Astral's mobility in the workplace. Beginning as a sales clerk selling yard goods, she rises to clerking in a department store; from that position she progresses to courses in typing and secretarial school; and from that post she moves to bookkeeping and a job in public works, where she meets Primus. He hires her to manage his real estate, a cluster of guest houses called Mile Trees Colony Hotel, which becomes her life's work. She remains his "keep Miss" throughout his marriage in a relationship that is known to the islanders and eventually to Primus's wife, Estelle.

Being manager of the hotel legitimizes a business association with Primus so that the personal relationship has a convenient foil. Although being the lover of an elected island politician enhances Astral's self-esteem, her position as a business manager is more fulfilling. She is an astute businessperson, as Primus recognizes, but her autonomy is limited and delusional, as is her dream of becoming Primus's wife and living in his big house. Class barriers collapse and reintegrate intermittently throughout the years of Astral's relationship with Primus. For example, when he brings his daughter to the hotel pool for her weekly swim, Astral, although she is property manager, is demoted to waitress by Primus's request that she serve his daughter juice after swimming. Astral exchanges herself for economic gain, altering her speech and clothing along the way to reflect her different class status. But because she lacks the status of wife, which would assure an equivalency of social class with her husband, Astral's situation is tenuous.[3]

In spite of the accoutrements of a position of authority and of Malvern's pleasure at her friend's increase in fortune, Astral is, in part, a victim of class and gender oppression. Moreover, she is socially isolated. Dressing up to visit Malvern and taking the bus to the slum where Malvern lives constitute her sole social outlets. Social intercourse with Primus is limited to sexual intercourse, which occurs during daylight hours at the property she manages because he makes it a point to be home at night with his wife and child. Astral is denied even the vicarious pleasure of unofficial wife status, since Primus neither talks to her about his life with Estelle nor takes Astral to their home when his wife is absent.

Astral's love for Primus and her long years of devotion to him amount to self-entrapment. Her victimization, gussied up in the appealing garb of social and economic advancement, conceals itself even from the victim. When Astral had an abortion at age eighteen, she had continued to feel "like that man on Drayton's Road left the damn wire thing up inside me" (182). Notably, Ursa's abortion, which produces an identical response, also prefigures loss and disillusionment. A significant difference in their outcomes, however, is that Astral, unlike Ursa, remains bound to an illusory autonomy whereas Ursa disconnects herself from Primus to gain authentic liberation.[4] Astral takes no literal journeys and her improved class status is self-deluding. Thus, she is psychically stymied and unable to travel toward a different self-definition.

Malvern's oppression, linked to economics and class, is merely the other side of the coin. She thinks of herself as "some little dark spot . . . that's gon have to take the first thing in a pair of pants to come along

and ask her a question" (121). She lives in a two-room house in the
slum called Armory Hill with her bus-driver husband. She has had
three children in five years and is again pregnant, often a characteristic
pattern in the experience of economically oppressed women. The constant pregnancies cause Malvern's physical deterioration, from being
"lean and sharp-boned" (176) to becoming a "motionless figure on the
bed . . . as inanimate as the pallet mattress under her . . . [who] won't
last the night" (366–67). Representative of many island women, she is
constrained by the vicious cycle of low wages, poor housing, and large
families. Her experience occupies a different region of the spectrum
of women's oppression; it is unlike Astral's, unlike that of the market
women who leave their hill shacks in the predawn hours for the long
trek to the market site, and unlike that of the prostitutes who await
the docking of military vessels. Among these experiences in *Daughters*,
Malvern's represents one of the many configurations shaping women's
oppression.

The oppressions most common to economically impoverished women
operate in Malvern's experience. She is woefully naive about the conspiracy of forces that seal her economic demise and that directly contribute to the poor health that will lead to her death. In spite of her
naivete and vicarious participation in Astral's class climbing, Malvern
finds pleasure in her securely defined roles of mother and wife. Her
satisfaction with family production must be tempered, however, by the
deplorable poverty in which they live and the conspiracy of forces responsible for it. Since she has no abortions, her life, metaphorically,
is not characterized by disillusion or loss. But she makes no journeys,
either metaphorically or literally, which means that personal growth is
unavailable to her.

Celeste Bellegarde, abandoned by a guardian cousin and literally left
at the Mackenzie store as one of the malnourished "doormouth children," begins a life of service at age eight, two months before Primus
Mackenzie's birth (157). Celeste illustrates an intriguing mix of personal service and self-definition. Grateful for food and shelter in her
destitution as a child, she serves the Mackenzie family without any apparent separate psychological existence. As a young servant, she sleeps

on a floor pallet in the room with Primus's sisters and becomes sexu-
ally involved with him, though only one brief narrative reference sub-
stantiates that occurrence: "Years later, she had only to touch herself
and there he would be again. . . . And not as some little seven- and
eight-years-old boy, but the PM grown and a man. . . . 'Oh, come
on, Celestine, there must have been someone. Some beau when you were
sweet sixteen.' Always teasing her, *oui*. Always thinking she had missed
out on something. What did [Estelle] know?" (348).

After Ursa's birth, Celeste continues as personal servant to Ursa and
Primus ("Her name is hardly out of his mouth before she isn't standing there" [166].) Her blanket approval of the adult Primus's behavior
and her silent criticism of Estelle's mothering of Ursa confirm Celeste's
devotion to both father and daughter. Her refusal to engage socially
with the family keeps her always within the periphery for servants.
One interpretation of Celeste's attitude and behavior is that they reflect
a cultural practice of keeping domestic service and interaction with the
employee strictly separate from each other. Another explanation is that
her acquiescence to her personal station is silent acknowledgment of a
power structure that relegates women to the status of depersonalized
workers in spite of Estelle's efforts to integrate her into outings with
the women in the family.

But Celeste's role in the narrative defies simple analysis. She is
clearly significant to Ursa's wholeness because of her prominence in the
girl's memory. When Ursa alters her physical appearance to reflect an
integrated self, Celeste, in part, is her model for the Caribbean component. Moreover, Celeste's sayings—instead of the words of Ursa's biological mother—reverberate in Ursa's head when she needs mothering.
In book 2, three of the chapters are narrated from Celeste's perspective;
in book 3, two chapters; and in book 4, one chapter. Celeste's narrative prominence underscores her self-possession, a prominent quality
of psychically whole ancestors in Marshall's novels. Celeste belongs
with this group—with Miss Thompson in *Brown Girl*, Carrington and
Leesy in *The Chosen Place*, and Aunt Cuney and Lebert Joseph in *Praisesong*. Nevertheless, her noncritical response to Primus and her blanket
negation of Estelle as mother and wife are problematic. Celeste's major

assets are selflessness and love in the service of the Mackenzie family, beginning with Primus's mother. Celeste exerts considerable influence on Ursa, helping to shape the Caribbean heritage in the growing girl's consciousness.

Daughters confirms that as a consequence of journeying, psychically whole women do not constitute a homogeneous population. Nevertheless, many of them are aware of a cultural connectedness among world communities of descendants of black Africa; as a result, their visions and responses, encompassing political, economical, and sociocultural agendas, are attuned to maelstroms of defeat in those communities. In *Daughters*, Estelle Mackenzie incorporates these qualities of psychic integration. Before her marriage and relocation to Triunion, she knows the island's history, particularly its legacy of insurgence. When Estelle gives birth to Ursa, she does not leave her daughter's bicultural heritage to chance but takes full advantage of situations that will ensure the daughter's knowledge and psychic well-being. For example, she educates Ursa about the island's history of resistance, and they visit the monument of local cultural heroes. Ursa, who comes of age in the Caribbean during the 1960s, wears the revolutionary Afro hair style and is raised in a home in which political and community involvement are valued. Especially notable are her mother's economic-reform efforts to assist female entrepreneurship on Triunion. While in high school, Ursa, sent to her grandparents' home in Connecticut, has contact with her uncle, a Freedom Rider in Alabama during the 1960s. Ursa's example, like Avatara's childhood visits to Tatem in *Praisesong*, suggests that psychic wellness in adulthood begins with certain kinds of preparation as a child. On Triunion, Estelle's attention to structuring an ordinary existence characterized by cultural immersion—instead of permitting the coddled, privileged one that Primus prefers—is intended to foster Ursa's independence rather than to produce a spoiled, class-conscious, dependent daughter.[5]

Ursa's increasing need to liberate herself from paternal domination is textually balanced by Viney's escalating concerns about maintaining her son's psychic balance in an urban environment. By the time this concern is necessary, Viney's own balance is secure, but she has also experienced her own need for liberation, not from her father but from her live-in lover of five years. Although she severs the relationship and orders him out of her apartment, her self-imposed guilt for failing to see his inutility influences her behavior for a significant period. It is a major part of her emotional trauma that climaxes in the pool incident that might have ended her life. Instead, near-drowning transmutes into psychic healing.[6] While Ursa is swimming, Viney "simply dangl[es] in the water . . . her arms outstretched along the ledge, holding onto it, and her head thrown all the way back" (76). She closes herself up metaphorically, as if she cannot see or hear. The threat of drowning is profoundly present as Viney, breaking her silence, begins "to heave like the tearful raging of a mute. . . . And there was this drag, this pull to her body. . . . Her outstretched arms were slowly sliding, slipping down. . . . One limp, fleshy arm slipped from the gutter, broke the skin of the water and disappeared" (79).

Holding her afloat, talking, and repeatedly screaming Viney's name, Ursa's voice finally penetrates, and "the weighted, near lifeless thing that was bearing her down with it suddenly started" (79). At this moment, Viney decides to embrace life and is spiritually reclaimed, as the circular dance performed on the Carriacou hillside was Avey Johnson's moment. Mary Lou Randour's research on women and spiritual transformation confirms that "a powerful sense of self" often "derives from the cleansing power of pain and fury," which describes Viney's circumstances (43). Embracing life as a spiritually invigorated woman Viney creates a family for herself (naming the son conceived through artificial insemination Robeson, after Paul, and later giving him a sister). She buys an old house in Brooklyn with a roomy backyard and performs much of its restoration with her own hands. She also involves herself in structuring the community where her children are growing up. Unlike Ursa, Viney does not find it necessary to resign from her corporate job, but it does not overwhelm her as Lowell Carruthers's job does to him.

Ursa deserves much of the credit for Viney's physical and psychic salvation as a result of this incident. While it is arguable whether Viney might have saved herself had she been alone in the pool, there are other literary examples of a friend's or ancestor's assistance in surviving trauma.[7] Ursa does not perform a traditional laying on of hands since they are in water, but her arms literally encircle Viney and keep her afloat until her transforming moment. In addition, Viney, along with a coerced Ursa ("Viney, you know I don't go in for all that spirituality stuff" [75]), has recently undergone initiation into a transcendental meditation group, though the counselor's advice seemingly has no applicability during Viney's trauma: "The woman [had] repeatedly whispered 'Ke'ram' in her ear. She was to say it silently with her eyes closed . . . at the beginning and end of each day, and whenever she felt the need" (76).

Perhaps more significant in Viney's salvation is the preparation for psychic wholeness evident in her background—a mother involved with children in her Petersburg, Virginia, community and a grandfather who had passed on to Viney his philosophy of evaluating people by their "usefulness" to the community. The near-drowning incident thus functions symbolically as a purging of the misdirection and ill judgment that has characterized Viney's life for the previous five years. In the same moment, a revitalized, psychically whole self is reborn, described textually as "Mother Daniels of Triumphant Baptist in Petersburg from the waist up and Buddha—legs folded lotus fashion—from the hips down" (83). Through this description, Viney becomes associated with the self-possession of maternal ancestors and the wisdom and perfect enlightenment of a deity (in addition to the spirituality of the meditation group).

The experiences of Ursa, Viney, and Estelle suggest that when a pattern of community and political involvement exists within a family, the possibilities are greater that the family's offspring acquires an incentive to politicize the personal, a component of wholeness, without having to endure individual trauma to earn it. In the experiences of Estelle, Ursa, and Viney, three kinds of community involvement are evident. In spite of "status disparity," Estelle operates primarily through political channels because of her liaison with a politician.[8] Her efforts with the arts council, however, are generated at the grass-roots level. In New Jersey, Ursa's focus on community is agency-related because her income-producing job is designed around community. Viney's community activism in Brooklyn, New York—not fully developed in the novel—moves in a different direction when a city policeman harasses her son for allegedly suspicious behavior. She seeks to have the police officer fired. Her activism, a representation of renewed necessity among African-American women whose roles have always included directing and protecting children, will indirectly benefit other boys whose psychic health is threatened by overzealous and brutal police behavior.

Ursa's liberation from her father as well as Viney and Estelle's mothering behavior suggests that psychically whole women are enablers for themselves, their children, and others. Being an enabler is perhaps the most crucial component of psychic wholeness because it means that the regenerative enterprise can be assisted in others. A self-enabled woman, while not immune to emotional trauma, is not destroyed by it. Spiritual wholeness engenders healing and survival that is self-initiated or originates outside self, as Ursa's, Viney's, and Estelle's examples illustrate. Their emotional traumas might have left them spiritually moribund, but they rebound and survive.

Amid Estelle's growing disillusionment with Primus's impotent governmental and economic reform, malicious gossip and anonymous telephone calls convince her that Primus maintains Astral Ford as his lover. Enraged by Primus's refusal to confirm or deny the allegations and obviously on the brink of an emotional abyss, Estelle leaves the house in the dead of night with her three-year-old daughter, drives to the end of the airport runway, and sits there, in Celeste's words, "like she's waiting for a airplane to come and crash into them, . . . sitting up in the car in her nightie and robe, the windows rolled up, all the doors locked and 'ti-Ursa still sleeping next to her on the seat. And you couldn't get a word out of her, *oui*. She acted like she din hear a thing you said. She refused even to look at you. Just staring off like a madwoman and holding the steering wheel like she thought the car was a airplane and could fly" (196).[9]

Primus's infidelity and his neutrality toward the accusations compel Estelle's most dramatic textual moment, which might have remained superimposed on her future behavior. Because she is psychically whole, however, this severe threat to her family's stability injures but does not devastate her. Although she is enabled through the immediate crisis of infidelity by the reasoned honesty of her friend and physician, his counsel merely allows her the space to marshal her reserves of spiritual endurance, and she is ultimately self-enabled through them. She heals without ongoing emotional injury to herself or to others around her. The full measure of Estelle's recovery is evidenced by her charity toward Astral Ford near the novel's end. Feeling sympathy for Astral's isolation and perhaps sensing the emptiness that Astral feels at the threatened sale of Mile Trees, Estelle urges Ursa to visit the other woman.

Similarly, Ursa's traumatic experience, choosing to privilege her Tri-union community over the bond between father and daughter, is a severe test of her spiritual wholeness and a delicate balancing enterprise for the author.[10] One of Marshall's techniques is the use of clothing to indicate a character's interior state, as when Merle Kinbona's eclectic dress indicates her spiritual disarray. Similarly, Ursa stops wearing the professional suits that mark her as a woman in a certain employment situation and replaces her relaxed hair with a braid like Celeste's. She gives up the kinds of possessions whose ownership compelled Avey and Jerome Johnson and Silla Boyce: a well-situated apartment, imported car, health-club membership, and prestigious job. These changes, made after a trip to the island, are motivated by Ursa's dissatisfaction with the economic and social welfare of the people there, and she connects the political state of the island with her father's party. Her response, however, is that of a psychically whole woman, adjusting certain parts of her exterior life to reflect her interior state.

Although Estelle's strategies for insuring her daughter's psychic well-being have succeeded, Ursa is still encumbered by her relationship with her father. Because she is psychically integrated, however, she is able to politicize the personal and in so doing to mobilize against her father to assist the Caribbean community. The liberation is not easy because Primus has practiced fatherhood with all the seriousness that the role deserves. His ideas of success for his adult daughter, however, are in conflict with her expressions of spiritual wholeness. It is difficult for Ursa to reconcile his personal and public spheres, but her social conscience can no longer ignore the deterioration that plagues the island in spite of her father's political office and his rhetoric about change. Divorcing her politics from her father's in effect rids her of the conflicts that have been unarticulated and that have prevented her presence on the island for four years.

Ursa's example offers the most comprehensive illustration of journeying beyond wholeness: One may possess the qualities of wholeness without complete personal freedom. Estelle's directing of Ursa's childhood and high school years fosters her independence. Ursa's rescuing of Viney and her termination of her relationship with Lowell Carruthers (who understood the bonds that she had to sever with her father but whose philosophy persistently differed from hers) are additional indicators of her psychic wholeness. In spite of positive decisions, however, peace eludes her, as is symbolized by the feeling that something remained of the aborted fetus. When that feeling terminates in pain after she exposes her father's complicity in the government scheme, she has achieved another level beyond wholeness. Ursa's example is perhaps the strongest proof that a psychically whole woman is a self-enabled woman who not only survives emotional trauma but ultimately heals herself.

Daughters illustrates women in various relationships to each other, in different stages of development, and in varying degrees of commitment to community.[11] Through Estelle, Viney, and Ursa, Marshall makes her best case for the postjourneying stage, which is to say that journeying never ceases. Spiritual wholeness neither assumes nor guarantees perfection. It broadens the arena for participation in personal and communal relationships because an essential identity grounded in cultural knowledge is secured. This is the focus of *Daughters*, Marshall's first posttrilogy novel, in which she moves beyond the process by which spiritual wholeness can be acquired to illustrate the difference that its possession can make.

NOTES

BIBLIOGRAPHY

INDEX

Notes

Introduction

1. See, for example, Leela Kapai, "Dominant Themes and Techniques in Paule Marshall's Fiction," *CLA Journal* 26 (1972): 49–59; Marcia Keizs, "Themes and Styles in the Works of Paule Marshall," *Negro American Literature Forum* 9 (1975): 67, 71–75; and Kimberly W. Benston, "Architectural Imagery and Unity in Paule Marshall's *Brown Girl, Brownstones*," *Negro American Literature Forum* 9 (1975): 67–70.

2. In the section on Marshall in *Black Women Novelists*, Barbara Christian subordinates the characters of *The Chosen Place* to the culture of Bournehills. She further equates the concept of time, both fluid and static, with the people and their culture, all rhythmically bound together (104–8).

3. In *There Is a River: The Black Struggle for Freedom in America* (New York: Vintage, 1983), Vincent Harding points out the euphemistic employment of the term "the Trade" to encapsulate the business of flesh stealing and selling in specific ports "from the Guinea coast to Barbados and Jamaica, to Charleston and Norfolk" (8).

4. Pettis, 123–24. Although Jean Carey Bond's review of *The Chosen Place* praises several features of the novel, it ignores the convergence of diaspora communities as one of the novel's primary components. Marshall's studied attention to communities of African descendants and her references to other displaced and exploited people connected by history and legacy are strangely omitted among a generally favorable review. See "Allegorical Novel by Talented Storyteller," *Freedomways* 10 (1970): 76–78.

5. See Joseph E. Holloway, ed., *Africanisms in American Culture* (Bloomington: Indiana Univ. Press, 1990). Margaret Washington Creel's essay, "Gullah Attitudes toward Life and Death" offers particularly pertinent information concerning com-

munity and spirituality that is reflected in Marshall's fiction and is useful for a conceptual analysis of *Praisesong* and *The Chosen People*.

Chapter 1: Generative Spaces: Paule Marshall's Imaginative Vision

1. Elaine Showalter takes credit for inventing the term *gynocritics* to describe the study of "women *as writers*. . . . Its subjects are the history, styles, themes, genres, and structures of writing by women; the psychodynamics of female creativity; the trajectory of the individual or collective female career; and the evolution and laws of a female literary tradition" (248). See "Feminist Criticism in the Wilderness," in *The New Feminist Criticism*, ed. Showalter, 243–70; and "Women's Time, Women's Space," 37.

2. Maya Angelou's *I Know Why the Caged Bird Sings* (1970) was nominated for a National Book Award; Alice Walker's *The Color Purple* (1982) was nominated for a National Book Critics Circle Award and won both the Pulitzer Prize and the American Book Award. Toni Morrison's *Song of Solomon* (1976) won the National Book Critics Circle Award; her *Beloved* (1987) won the New York State Governor's Art Award, the Pulitzer Prize, the Robert F. Kennedy Award and was nominated for the National Book Award and the National Book Critics Circle Award. Gloria Naylor's *The Women of Brewster Place* (1983) won the American Book Award.

3. Most critics have identified the coming-of-age theme as the most compelling subject in *Brown Girl*. See, for example, Eugenia Collier, "Selina's Journey Home: From Alienation to Unity in Paule Marshall's *Brown Girl, Brownstones*," *Obsidian* 8 (1982): 6–19; Sandra Y. Govan, "Women within the Circle: Selina and Silla Boyce," *Callaloo* 18 (1983): 148–52; Geta J. Leseur, "*Brown Girl, Brownstones* as a Novel of Development"; and Rosalie Riegle Troester, "Turbulence and Tenderness: Mothers, Daughters, and 'Othermothers' in Paule Marshall's *Brown Girl, Brownstones*," *Sage* 1 (1984): 13–16.

4. Identifying a relationship between black women's fiction and their confrontation with history, Susan Willis emphasizes that Marshall's work uses history as it has affected black women's lives in both private and public spheres. See particularly the first chapter in *Specifying*. Hortense Spillers argues convincingly in "Cross-Currents" that discontinuity represents a compelling feature among black women's texts, but she also discovers that historical reference constitutes a "most consistent comparison" among books published from 1965 (Margaret Walker) to Marshall's *Praisesong*.

5. Richard Yarborough places the ideology of the American dream in the context of black American history in a discussion of three novels. See "The Quest for the American Dream in Three Afro-American Novels: *If He Hollers Let Him Go, The Street*, and *Invisible Man*," MELUS 8 (1981): 33–59.

6. Washington, " 'The Darkened Eye,' " 33. The exclusion that Washington documents receives support in Charles Johnson's *Being and Race*, where his list of "major" writers of the 1940s and '50s—"a full generation of writers"—is all male, as is his list of writers inspired by Wright's *Native Son* (12–13). See also Jacqueline Jones, 311.

7. Bell's use of statements by Toni Cade Bambara and Mary Helen Washington fails to strengthen his argument. Rather than "underscoring problematics" of the tradition, both Bambara and Washington merely point out obvious differences in the fiction of black men and women.

8. See, for example, Daryl Dance, ed., *Fifty Caribbean Writers: A Bio-Bibliographical and Critical Source Book* (Westport: Greenwood, 1986); Jeniphier R. Carnegie, "Selected Bibliography of Criticism and Related Works," in *Out of the Kumbla*, ed. Carole Boyce Davies and Elaine Savory Fido (Trenton, N.J.: African World Press, 1990), 373–94.

9. Marshall speaks about her interest in the history of black people and of its role in her fiction in various interviews. Refer to "Return of a Native Daughter: An Interview with Paule Marshall and Maryse Conde," trans. John Williams, *Sage* 3 (1986): 52–53; see also Marshall, "Shaping the World of My Art," *New Letters* 40 (1973): 97–112.

Chapter 2: An Absence of Wholeness: Negotiating Community in the Strategy of Survival

1. Ann R. Morris and Margaret M. Dunn make a connection between the land and one's mother and a woman's progress toward self identification and fulfillment. If no mother-daughter relationship exists, then the mother's land itself may become a substitute, a phenomenon that the authors identify in some Caribbean women's work, including *The Chosen Place*. See " 'The Bloodstream of our Inheritance': Female Identity and the Caribbean Mothers' Land" in *Motherlands: Black Women's Writing from Africa, the Caribbean and South Asia*. ed. Susheila Nasta, 219–37. New Brunswick: Rutgers Univ. Press, 1992.

2. Maroons, like slaves throughout the New World, rejected plantation deprivation and sought freedom in spite of its hazards. Maroonage, according to Hilary Beckles, was the "most common expression of discontent" with enslavement. Maroon societies, found in the Leeward Islands during the early sugar era, presented serious problems for the administration in the southern hills of Antigua as early as the seventeenth century. Barbados, unlike Jamaica, did not have the hilly terrain that would facilitate viable maroon culture. See Beckles, *Black Rebellion in Barbados: The Struggle Against Slavery, 1627–1838* (Bridgetown, Barbados: Antilles Publications, 1984).

3. Community as a physical place defined by its black population as essentially separate from the dominant culture has consistently been a prominent feature of African-American literature. Examples of this phenomenon include Ernest Gaines, who sets his novels in black areas of rural Louisiana; Gloria Naylor in her depictions of Brewster Place, Linden Hills (in the novels that incorporate those names), and Willow Springs (in *Mama Day*), and Toni Morrison's setting for *Sula, Song of Solomon, Tar Baby,* and *Beloved.* Elizabeth A. Schultz examines community in several African-American novels in "The Insistence Upon Community in the Contemporary Afro-American Novel," *College English* 41 (1979): 170–84.

4. A provocative passiveness is also apparent in Leesy in *The Chosen Place,* who disdains technological marvels (the Opel that Vere transforms into a race/death car). (Apparatus for processing sugarcane had previously killed her husband.) Both Da-Duh and Leesy, solidly attuned to the productions of nature, intuitively understand the dangers of mechanization, but curiously, they do not act to save their loved ones from it.

5. Carole Boyce Davies analyzes "To Da-Duh, in Memoriam" placing emphasis on "ancestry and youth, tradition and modernity." She particularly values the New York child's rejection of the canefields as "an important departure from that particular experience and history" (61).

6. The discussion of maintaining distance between physical place and psychological space as a key concept in Marshall's canon occurs in the analysis of *Praisesong for the Widow* in chapter 4. See Creel, "Gullah Attitudes."

7. Carolyn Cooper quotes Erna Brodber's provocative statement concerning the difference between history in books and what the islanders acknowledge as their more representative history. See Brodber, "Oral Sources and the Creation of a Social History of the Caribbean," *Jamaica Journal* 16 (1983): 2–11.

8. In "Chosen Place, Timeless People," Hortense Spillers discusses Harriet only as a component of the Merle-Saul-Harriet triangle. In *Black Women Novelists,* Barbara Christian's lengthy summary of Harriet's character (121–27) focuses on her roles as wife and determined helpmate. Christian contends that Harriet's inability to learn from Bournehills offers some insight into the uses to which Marshall puts her character.

9. See Benjamin Ray's discussion of cyclical time, posited as the special nature of ritual time, in *African Religions*: "In this respect, ritual time is an interruption of ordinary linear time, a time-out-of-time, when man may reestablish contact with the creative events of the cosmogonic period. In ritual, the mythical past is thus constantly recoverable" (41).

10. A sense of history as a viable determinant in the lives of characters who are conscious of the intersections of past and present is apparent in several novels by women writers, aside from those that are obviously anchored in historical moments

such as Morrison's *Beloved* or Sherley Anne Williams's *Dessa Rose*. Consider, for example, the interplay between the texts of history and memory in Gloria Naylor's *Mama Day* and *Linden Hills*. Susan Straight's *I Been in Sorrow's Kitchen and Licked Out All the Pots*, a novel anchored in the distinctive African-American experience in the sea islands and Charleston, South Carolina, incorporates a historical component in the form of the present generation seeking clues to the past through gravestones and photographs.

11. Trudier Harris writes one of the most extensive discussions of Cuffee Ned and his value to the community in "Three Black Women Writers and Humanism: A Folk Perspective," in *Black American Literature and Humanism*, ed. R. Baxter Miller (Lexington: Univ. Press of Kentucky, 1981), 50–74. The values that Cuffee Ned posits in Bournehills are more useful to the people than the limitations of organized Christian religion.

12. Beckles, *Black Rebellion*, cites an islandwide rebellion organized by a slave Cuffee but discovered before its execution in May 1675.

13. Bournehills is structured by several significant holidays other than carnival, Easter, and Christmas, including First Bank Holiday, a celebration of the Emancipation, in August and All Souls Day, an all-night service at the graveyard in November. Of these holidays, only Whitsuntide, the race in Spiretown in which Vere crashes his car, and carnival receive emphasis in the novel.

14. Toni Morrison's *Song of Solomon* contains an organizing ritual that builds community and male camaraderie in a manner similar to the hog killing in *The Chosen Place*. When Milkman Dead enters the Virginia community of Shalimar as an arrogant outsider, he must fight, literally, because he offends with his city presumptions. After the fight, as an enterprise of reconciliation, the men take Milkman, a complete novice with the gun, on a hunt. After they shoot and kill a bobcat, they skin and clean it and give its heart to Milkman. Like the hog killing, this hunt solidifies the men as a group.

15. Gerald Prince defines referential code as the voice in which a narrative refers to a given cultural background. This term seems particularly applicable to the relationship between Estelle and Ursa. Each relocates to a different community with different cultural experiences, yet they share a similar historical context. Their modes of interaction with their new communities, rely, in part, on their reciprocal cultural experiences, thereby enabling effective community juxtaposition in *Daughters*. For discussion of referential code, see Gerald Prince, *Dictionary of Narratology* (Lincoln: Univ. of Nebraska Press, 1987), 80.

Chapter 3: The Pernicious Triad: The Dynamics of Race, Class, and Gender in the Quest for Wholeness

1. Barbara Christian develops the idea of reflective properties in Marshall's characters and their physical community in *The Black Woman Novelist*.

2. In "Race and Class Exploitation," Howard McGary, Jr., points out that some theorists maintain that capitalism is nonexploitative, because although it may allow or encourage taking advantage of others, such practices are not unjust.

3. Research on the criteria for middle-class status in the black and white communities indicates differences in perception. Sociologists Lynn Weber Cannon and Reeve Vannemon point out studies that emphasize status, respect, prestige, and esteem as "critical evaluative dimensions in the Black community." They suggest that possessing middle-class values about education or engaging in selected public behaviors amounts to being middle class. However, Cannon and Vannemon's findings differ from what they term "liberal definitions" of middle-class status. They conclude that work requiring intellect versus work involving manual labor best sums up the difference between perceptions of middle class and working class, although " 'front,' 'respectability,' and other status concerns may hold importance." They emphasize the integration of race, class, and gender into an analysis of a wide range of behaviors and attitudes because to omit them produces a "distorted view of social reality." See "Class Perceptions in the Black Community," Center for Research on Women, Memphis State University.

4. *Heading* is carrying an extremely heavy load of cut cane atop the head. Marshall centers her graphic description of this essential work on Gwen, thus emphasizing its physical demands on women. See Wilkinson.

5. Trudier Harris cites Silla's capitalist philosophy, her enticement by the American dream, and her alienation from southern blacks as among her destructive behaviors. Harris judges her as being in a perpetual state of the blues. See "No Outlet for the Blues: Silla Boyce's Plight in *Brown Girl, Brownstones*," *Callaloo* 6 (1983): 57–67.

6. See Jones, 163–70, for a detailed statistical discussion of the plight of black northern and southern women domestic workers before World War II and in the factories during the war.

7. It is ironic that the grueling work of harvesting sugarcane awaited the young men who emigrated from the islands in search of economic stability. The environment was often hazardous, as in mosquito-infested areas in Panama.

8. Alec Wilkinson calls harvesting sugarcane "the most perilous work in America." Because gloves are expensive and wear out quickly cutters work without them. Their hands blister, callus, and stiffen, becoming "like lineoleum" and taking "weeks to return to usefulness" (3).

9. Claudia Mitchell-Kernan's essay, "Signifying, Loud-Talking, and Marking," offers an extensive discussion of verbal behaviors specific to the black community. See also the essays of Grace Sims Holt, Roger D. Abrahams, and William Labov in Thomas Kochman, ed., *Rappin' and Stylin' Out: Communication in Urban Black America* (Urbana: Univ. of Illinois Press, 1972).

10. According to Gates, texts engage in signifying with one another just as individuals do. His recognition of the transfer of a linguistic practice from the black community to a literary text parallels this section's focus on the use of forms of talk in literary texts. See also Geneva Smitherman, *Talkin and Testifyin*, for examples of dialogue from Chester Himes's *Cotton Comes to Harlem* (122–23), Ralph Ellison's *Invisible Man* (131), and Richard Wright's short story, "Big Boy Leaves Home" (135), that reflect verbal traditions in black communities.

11. This linguistic continuity is the "unbroken arc of metaphysical presupposition and patterns of figuration shared through space and time among black cultures in West Africa, South America, the Caribbean, and in the United States," for which Gates argues in recognizing the pervasiveness of the trickster figure in black culture. See *Figures in Black*, 237. Mae Gwendolyn Henderson similarly acknowledges "the notion of community among those who share a common history, language, and culture" (120).

12. Marshall explores the subject of talk in promoting intimacy among women in "From the Poets in the Kitchen," in *Reena and Other Stories*, 2–12.

13. Fiction by black women writers abounds in its depictions of women's talk used to foster self-definition and to offer protection from the callous external world. See, for example, the exchanges of Silla and her female friends as well as those of Selina and Beryl in Marshall's *Brown Girl*, Janie's narrative to Phoeby in Zora Neale Hurston's *Their Eyes Were Watching God*, and the conversations between Nell and Sula in Toni Morrison's *Sula*.

14. In *Slave Women in Caribbean Society*, Barbara Bush cites a major danger inherent in oppression and adjustment: "If slaves failed to resist the process of alienation which was inherent in the slave system, they faced 'psychic annihilation.' The preservation of cultural identity was paramount to survival" (7). Although Merle is not enslaved, slavery's disabling structures persist: psychic fracturing is one of the consequences.

15. Among the characters in fiction by black women who experience madness and commit or attempt murder are Eva Medina in Gayl Jones's *Eva's Man* and Myrna in Alice Walker's short story, "Really, Doesn't Crime Pay?" in her collection *In Love and Trouble*.

16. Pecola Breedlove in Toni Morrison's *The Bluest Eye*, Hagar in Morrison's *Song of Solomon*, and Eva Medina in Gayl Jones's *Eva's Man* are all victims of insanity. The absence of communal support structures contributes to Pecola's and

Eva's problems; Hagar, in spite of women's kinship bonds, becomes a victim of madness beyond help.

Chapter 4: The Journey Completed: Spiritual Regeneration in *Praisesong for the Widow*

1. See also Francis Smith Foster, "Changing Concepts of the Black Woman," *Journal of Black Studies* 3 (1973): 433–54; Mae C. King, "The Politics of Sexual Stereotypes," *The Black Scholar* (1973): 12–23; and Collins, *Black Feminist Thought*, 43–66.

2. There are several clusters of novels, some of which are discussed in this book, in which conflicts that imperil women may be read as an indictment of the dominant culture's construction of gender and devaluation of blacks. In Jessie Fauset's *Plum Bun*, for example, Euro-American culture is prioritized and the desire to pass is prominent not only because women in the 1920s passively viewed themselves in the reflection of men but also because there were few opportunities for economic advancement that existed for unmarried black women. Issues of class and self-worth inform behavioral decisions in texts as diverse as Gwendolyn Brooks's "Maud Martha" and Dorothy West's *The Living Is Easy*.

3. Ann Scarboro uses *psychological reintegration* in "The Healing Process: A Paradigm for Self-Renewal in Paule Marshall's *Praisesong for the Widow* and Camara Laye's *Le Regard du roi*," *Modern Language Studies* 19 (1989): 28–36.

4. This phrase is borrowed from *The Huddled Masses*, Time Life Video, 1972. Although this videotape covers immigrant populations in the United States, it contains virtually no information on West Indians settling in New York or elsewhere in the United States.

5. Walker's discussion of her grandmother's role affirms how the female ancestor's presence is felt in private lives and offered in fiction. Walker's experience is a powerful example of an ancestor passing on family and cultural history to new generations. See Walker, *How I Wrote* Jubilee (Chicago: Third World Press, 1972).

6. For two recent discussions of the ancestral presence as a mediating force in contemporary black women's literature, see Holloway, 112–40, and Wilentz, 81–115.

7. In "Three Black Women Writers and Humanism: A Folk Perspective," Trudier Harris differentiates between Christianity and humanism in Mariah Upshure's strategies for survival. Although Harris finds both concepts vital in Mariah's life, Christianity is more an empty form than humanism is, because the latter provides substantive behavioral guides for negotiating the daily physical world in which black people live. Harris cites "folk ancestors" (57) as having created these behavioral guides, but for Mariah the ancestors constitute remote forebears rather than close members of her family.

8. Explaining the genesis of *Praisesong* and her preoccupation with the story of the Ibos, Marshall has identified the Georgia Writers' Project–Works Progress Administration's *Drums and Shadows* as the source of the tale. Interestingly, *Daughters of the Dust*, a film written and directed by Julie Dash and released by Kino International in 1992, uses the Ibo story as it appears in *Praisesong*. Set on the South Carolina sea islands, the film concerns a family whose members plan to move to the city and the female elder's fear that they will subsequently lose their traditional island culture.

9. Ebele O. Eko views each of the four sections of *Praisesong* as corresponding to an epoch in African-American history. She equates "Sleeper's Wake" with the "historic cultural and literary awakening of American Blacks and . . . Blacks everywhere, through the Harlem Renaissance. It recalls parallel movements like Negritude and [the] Haitian Renaissance in Africa and the diaspora." Such an epoch awakens people to Karl Marx's essential truth "that a people without history can easily be persuaded" (145).

10. In *Song of Solomon*, Toni Morrison connects Milkman solidly with the earth at a strategic point in his self-discovery—as he descends the hilly terrain with his new kinsmen after the hunt for the bobcat. In other works, Marshall, too, connects physical stability, emotional wholeness (though it might be temporary), and the earth, particularly in her descriptions of Vere in *The Chosen Place* after he has danced at carnival and of the young servant girl in "Barbados."

11. I am indebted to Jerry Barrax, my colleague at North Carolina State University, for pointing out to me the definition of *Avatara*. Marshall admits to having had difficulty in choosing her protagonist's name: she was Ursa or Vernel through several drafts before Marshall thought of Jean Toomer's Avey in *Cane*. The author knew that Avey could be a shortened form of Avatara and that she could be creative with this black woman's name, as African Americans often are in their naming processes (Marshall, lecture). The essential similarity between Toomer's and Marshall's dissimilar women is that Toomer's Avey holds a part of herself sacrosanct, the lesson that Marshall's Avey learns from the story of the Ibos.

12. This chapter will not attempt a detailed comparison of Milkman's and Avatara's quests, but their journeys are complementary and in accord with Joseph Campbell's explanation of mythic quests. The divergence in their expressions of spiritual wholeness represents gendered behavior. For a comparison of Avatara Johnson and Milkman Dead, see Joyce Pettis, "Narrative Magic: Myth, Quests, and Renewals in Paule Marshall's *Praisesong for the Widow* and Toni Morrison's *Song of Solomon*" (paper presented at the international meeting of the Popular Culture Association, King Alfred's College, Winchester, England, July 1991).

Chapter 5: *Daughters:* Some Consequences of Journeying

1. Gikandi's and similar statements that black women have been excluded from public life are only partially true: research reveals black women's community activism and club movements designed to benefit community. Such activism, while public, has not always received national attention. Paula Gidding's *When and Where I Enter* provides an introductory discussion of black American women's political involvement in their communities. In the postcolonial context, Jessie Bernard raises questions about women in Third World countries who organize to assist political change only to find the promises that accompanied and sometimes justified their efforts ignored. See *The Female World from a Global Perspective* (Bloomington: Indiana Univ. Press, 1987), 68–87. Hazel V. Carby, *Reconstructing Womanhood* (New York: Oxford Univ. Press, 1987), also discusses black women's national involvement in nineteenth-century life. She points out that "female intellectual activity at both an individual and a collective level has remained invisible, subsumed under the wealth of research into the ideas and actions of male leaders, thinkers, and activists" (84).

2. As in her other fiction, Marshall includes a number of male figures in *Daughters.* Because they are not pivotal players in the illustration of spiritual wholeness, however, they are discussed in another context in chapter 2.

3. Christine Dephy offers a provocative discussion of the relationship among class, husbands, and wives in *Close to Home: A Materialist Analysis of Women's Oppression,* trans. Diana Leonard (Amherst: Univ. of Massachusetts Press, 1984), 35–39. She points out obvious inconsistencies and inequities in social-stratification theory when occupation is a consideration in class stratification. Nonworking wives are automatically situated in the class of their husbands, as are working wives, regardless of what kind of work they do. Yet a man is never classified according to his wife's work.

4. Chapter 2 contains a more detailed discussion of the symbolic importance of abortions in this novel.

5. I am indebted to Carol Marsh Lockett of the English department at Georgia State University for a significant insight concerning Estelle's mothering of Ursa. In sending her daughter to the United States, Estelle in effect liberates Ursa from the influences of the girl's father. In so doing, she denies Ursa that role so that the responsibility for self-liberation is delayed until it is dramatized during the elections.

6. Viney's trauma is occasioned not solely by the breakup of her five-year relationship but also by her lack of insight. When she has become sufficiently disillusioned with Willie Jenkins and asks that he leave her apartment, he moves in with a white man in the same building. Viney blames herself for not recognizing Jenkins's bisexuality.

7. Marshall strongly implies that a pattern of community service in families influences their offspring, for example, Estelle's mother's and brother's activism in Connecticut, Primus's and Estelle's involvement in Triunion, and Ursa's community-based occupation in New Jersey.

8. Bernard uses the term *status disparity* in writing about the hierarchical relationship of American and European women with Third World women (118–19), particularly because the Third World women are often in service roles. In *Daughters*, although Celeste disparingly refers to Estelle as the "blanche neg," Estelle does not encounter the problem of status disparity because she does not perceive the community as Other or as an opponent. As a psychically whole woman, she understands how Triunion and her black Connecticut community are components of the African diaspora.

9. The "statues" poses that Estelle assumes offer another example of a highly dramatized moment of emotional retreat while she collects herself. See chapter 2 for a fuller discussion of this topic.

10. In an interview with Daryl Cumber Dance, Marshall spoke extensively about her motivations and objectives in writing *Daughters*. She admitted to a connection between her relationship with her father and Ursa's need to liberate herself from Primus's domination. Marshall has worked to liberate herself from the memory of the bitterness and outrage caused by her father's desertion of her family (to join Father Divine's cult), work that took many years. One cannot overlook another connection with Marshall's father: Deighton Boyce in *Brown Girl* joined the Father's group and similarly abandoned his family, leaving a devastated Selina to painfully reconstruct herself.

11. See Sandra A. Zagarell, "Narrative of Community: The Identification of a Genre," *Signs* 13 (1988): 498–527. Zagarell examines several nineteenth- and twentieth-century narratives to argue for the existence of a new genre that she calls narratives of community. She believes that "the self exists here as part of the interdependent network of community rather than as an individualistic unit." This connection constitutes a "coherent response to the industrialism, urbanization, and the spread of capitalism" (499).

Bibliography

Abrahams, Roger D. "An American Vocabulary of Celebrations." In *Time Out of Time: Essays on the Festival,* ed. Alessandro Falassi, 173–83. Albuquerque: Univ. of New Mexico Press, 1987.

——— . "The Training of the Man of Words in Talking Sweet." In *Verbal Art as Performance,* ed. Richard Bauman, 117–32. Rowley, Mass.: Newbury House, 1977.

Akbar, Na'im. "Chains and Images of Psychological Slavery." In *Readings from a Black Perspective,* ed. Carolyn M. Dejoie, 13–28. Madison: Health and Human Services. Univ. of Wisconsin, 1985.

Asante, Molefi Kete. *The Afrocentric Idea.* Philadelphia: Temple Univ. Press, 1987.

Awkward, Michael. *Inspiriting Influences: Tradition, Revision, and Afro-American Women's Novels.* New York: Columbia Univ. Press, 1989.

Baldwin, Joseph A. "African Self Consciousness and the Mental Health of African Americans." *Journal of Black Studies* 15 (1984): 177–94.

——— . "Psychological Aspects of European Cosmology in American Society." *Western Journal of Black Studies* 9 (1985): 216–23.

Bambara, Toni Cade. *The Salt Eaters.* New York: Random House, 1981.

Bell, Bernard. *The Afro-American Novel and Its Tradition.* Amherst: Univ. of Massachusetts Press, 1987.

——— . "Ann Petry's Demythologizing of American Culture and Afro-American Character." In *Conjuring: Black Women, Fiction, and Literary Tradition,* ed. Majorie Pryse and Hortense Spillers, 105–15. Bloomington: Indiana Univ. Press, 1985.

Blauner, Robert. "Colonized and Immigrant Minorities." In *From Different Shores: Perspectives on Race and Ethnicity in America,* ed. Ronald Takaki, 149–60. New York: Oxford Univ. Press, 1987.

Brathwaite, Edward. "Rehabilitations: West Indian History and Society in the Art of Paule Marshall's Novel." *Caribbean Studies* 10 (1970): 125–34.

——. "West Indian History and Society in the Art of Paule Marshall's Novels." *Journal of Black Studies* 1 (1970): 225–28.

Brooks, Gwendolyn. "Maud Martha." In *Blacks*, 141–60. 1953; Chicago: The David Company, 1987.

Brown, Lloyd. "The Rhythms of Power in Paule Marshall's Fiction." *Novel* 7 (1974): 159–67.

Bush, Barbara. *Slave Women in Caribbean Society, 1650–1838*. Bloomington: Indiana Univ. Press, 1990.

Campbell, Joseph. *The Hero with a Thousand Faces*. 2d ed. Princeton, N.J.: Princeton Univ. Press, 1968.

Childress, Alice. "A Candle in a Gale Wind." In *Black Women Writers, 1950–1980*, ed. Mari Evans, 111–16. New York: Anchor Press, 1984.

Christ, Carol P., and Judith Plaskow. *WomanSpirit Rising*. San Francisco: Harper and Row, 1979.

Christian, Barbara. *Black Women Novelists: The Development of a Tradition, 1892–1976*. Westport, Conn.: Greenwood, 1980.

——. "Ritualistic Process and the Structure of Paule Marshall's *Praisesong for the Widow*. In *Black Feminist Criticism: Perspectives on Black Women Writers*, 149–58. New York: Pergamon, 1985.

Clifton, Lucille. *Generations: A Memoir*. New York: Random House, 1976.

Collier, Eugenia. "The Closing of the Circle: Movement from Division to Wholeness in Paule Marshall's Fiction." In *Black Women Writers, 1950–1980*, ed. Mari Evans, 295–315. New York: Anchor Press, 1984.

Collins, Patricia Hill. *Black Feminist Thought*. Boston: Unwin Hyman, 1990.

——. "The Social Construction of Black Feminist Thought." *Signs* 14 (1989): 875–84.

Cooper, Carolyn. "The Oral Witness and the Scribal Document: Divergent Acts of Slavery in Two Novels of Barbados." In *West Indian Literature and its Social Content*, ed. Mark McWatt, 3–11. St. Michael, Barbados: Department of English, Univ. of the West Indies, Cave Hill, 1985.

Crane, Michael. *Testing the Chains: Resistance to Slavery in the British West Indies*. Ithaca, N.Y.: Cornell Univ. Press, 1982.

Creel, Margaret Washington. "Gullah Attitudes toward Life and Death." In *Africanisms in American Culture*, ed. Joseph E. Holloway, 69–97. Bloomington: Indiana Univ. Press, 1990.

Crocker, Christopher. "Ritual and the Development of Social Structure: Liminality and Inversion." In *The Roots of Ritual*, ed. James D. Shaughnessy, 47–86. Grand Rapids, Mich.: William B. Eerdmans Publishing Co., 1973.

Cudjoe, Selwyn R. *Resistance and Caribbean Literature*. Athens: Ohio Univ. Press, 1980.

Dance, Daryl Cumber. "An Interview with Paule Marshall." *Southern Review* 28 (1992): 1–20.

Davies, Carole Boyce. "Writing Home: Gender and Heritage in the Works of Afro-Caribbean/American Women Writers." In *Out of the Kumbla: Caribbean Women and Literature*, ed. Carol Boyce Davies and Elaine Savory Fido, 59–74. Trenton, N.J.: African World Press, 1990.

Deane, Seamus. Introduction to *Nationalism, Colonialism, and Literature*, by Terry Eagleton, Fredric Jameson, and Edward Said. Minneapolis: Univ. of Minnesota Press, 1990.

Dennison, Dorothy Lee Hamer. "Cultural Reclamation: The Development of Pan-African Sensibility in the Fiction of Paule Marshall." Ph.D. diss., Brown Univ., 1983.

de Weever, Jacqueline. *Mythmaking and Metaphor in Black Women's Fiction*. New York: St. Martin's Press, 1991.

Dickerson, Vanessa D. "The Property of Being in Paule Marshall's *Brown Girl, Brownstones*." *Obsidian II* 6 (1991): 1–13.

Dill, Bonnie Thornton. "The Dialectics of Black Womanhood." *Signs* 4 (1979): 543–55.

Dixon, Melvin. *Ride Out the Wilderness: Geography and Identity in Afro-American Literature*. Urbana: Univ. of Illinois Press, 1987.

Donovan, Josephine. *Feminist Theory: The Intellectual Traditions of American Feminism*. New York: Frederick Ungar, 1985.

Eisenstein, Zillah. *Capitalist Patriarchy*. New York: Monthly Review Press, 1979.

Eko, Ebelo O. "Oral Tradition: The Bridge to Africa in Paule Marshall's *Praisesong for the Widow*." *Western Journal of Black Studies* 10 (1986): 143–47.

Fanon, Frantz. *The Wretched of the Earth*. Trans. Constance Farrington. New York: Grove Weidenfeld, 1963.

Fauset, Jessie. *Plum Bun*. 1928; Boston: Beacon Press, 1990.

Gabbin, Joanne V. "A Laying on of Hands: Black Women Writers Exploring the Roots of Their Folk and Cultural Tradition." In *Wild Women in the Whirlwind: Afra-American Culture and the Contemporary Literary Renaissance*, ed. Joanne M. Braxton and Andree Nicola McLaughlin, 246–63. New Brunswick, N.J.: Rutgers Univ. Press, 1990.

Gates, Henry Louis, Jr. *Figures in Black: Words, Signs, and the "Racial" Self*. New York: Oxford Univ. Press, 1987.

———. "Frederick Douglass and the Language of the Self." *Yale Review* 70 (1981): 592–611.

Georgia Writers' Project–Works Progress Administration. *Drums and Shadows:*

Survival Studies among the Georgia Coastal Negroes. Athens: Univ. of Georgia Press, 1940.

Giddings, Paula. *When and Where I Enter: The Impact of Black Women on Race and Sex in America.* New York: William Morrow, 1984.

Gikandi, Simon. *Writing in Limbo: Modernism and Caribbean Literature.* Ithaca, N.Y.: Cornell Univ. Press, 1992.

Hamerow, Theodore S. *Reflections on History and Historians.* Madison: Univ. of Wisconsin Press, 1987.

Harris, Trudier. *From Mammies to Militants: Domestics in Black American Literature.* Philadelphia: Temple Univ. Press, 1982.

Henderson, Mae Gwendolyn. "Speaking in Tongues: Dialogics, Dialectics, and the Black Woman Writer's Literary Tradition." In *Reading Black, Reading Feminist,* ed. Henry Louis Gates, Jr., 116–42. New York: Penguin, 1990.

Henderson, Stephen. Introduction to *Black Women Writers, 1950–1980,* ed. Mari Evans. New York: Anchor Books, 1984.

Hoetink, H. "Race and Color in the Caribbean." In *Caribbean Contours,* ed. Sidney W. Mintz and Sally Price, 55–84. Baltimore: John Hopkins Univ. Press, 1985.

Holloway, Karla. *Moorings and Metaphors.* New Brunswick: Rutgers Univ. Press, 1992.

Hunter, Kristin. *God Bless the Child.* 1964; Washington, D.C.: Howard Univ. Press, 1986.

Hurston, Zora Neale. *Their Eyes Were Watching God.* Urbana: Univ. of Illinois Press, 1978.

Jackson, Gerald Gregory. "Black Psychology: An Avenue to the Study of Afro-Americans." *Journal of Black Studies* 12 (1982): 241–60.

Johnson, Charles. *Being and Race: Black Writing since 1970.* Bloomington: Indiana Univ. Press, 1988.

Jones, Gayl. *Corregidora.* New York: Random House, 1975.

———. *Eva's Man.* 1976; Boston: Beacon Press, 1987.

Jones, Jacqueline. *Labor of Love, Labor of Sorrow: Black Women, Work, and the Family, from Slavery to the Present.* New York: Vintage Books, 1985.

King, Deborah K. "Multiple Jeopardy, Multiple Consciousness: The Context of a Black Feminist Ideology." *Signs* 14 (1988): 42–72.

Kochman, Thomas. "Toward an Ethnography of Black American Speech Behavior." In *Rappin' and Stylin' Out: Communication in Urban Black America,* ed. Thomas Kochman, 241–64. Urbana: Univ. of Illinois Press, 1972.

Kramarae, Cheris. *Women and Men Speaking.* Rowley, Mass.: Newbury House, 1981.

Kubitschek, Missy Dehn. *Claiming the Heritage: African-American Women Novelists and History.* Jackson: Univ. Press of Mississippi, 1991.

Kwabena Nketia, J. H. "The Musical Heritage of Africa." In *Slavery, Colonialism, and Racism*, ed. Sidney W. Mintz, 151–62. New York: W. W. Norton, 1974.

Leseur, Geta J. "*Brown Girl, Brownstones* as a Novel of Development." *Obsidian II* 1 (1986): 119–29.

McDowell, Deborah. " 'The Changing Same': Generational Connections and Black Women Novelists." *New Literary History* 18 (1987): 281–302.

———. "New Directions for Black Feminist Criticism." In *Feminist Criticism*, ed. Elaine Showalter, 186–99. New York: Pantheon Books, 1985.

McGary, Howard, Jr. "Race and Class Exploitation." In *Exploitation and Exclusion: Race and Class in Contemporary U.S. Society*, 14–27. London: Hans Zell Publishers, 1991.

Marshall, Paule. *Brown Girl, Brownstones*. 1959; New York: Feminist Press, 1981.

———. *The Chosen Place, The Timeless People*. 1969; New York: Vintage, 1984.

———. Lecture presented at a conference, "Looking Back with Pleasure: The Life of Olaudah Equiano," Salt Lake City, October 1989.

———. *Daughters*. New York: Atheneum, 1991.

———. *Praisesong for the Widow*. New York: Putnam, 1983.

———. *Reena and Other Stories*. New York: Feminist Press, 1983.

———. *Soul Clap Hands and Sing*. 1961; Washington, D.C.: Howard Univ. Press, 1988.

Mead, Margaret. "Ritual and Social Crisis." In *Roots of Ritual*, ed. James D. Shaughnessy, 87–101. Grand Rapids, Mich.: William B. Eerdmans, 1973.

Minar, Davis, and Scott Greer. *The Concept of Community*. Chicago: Aldine Publishing Co., 1969.

Mitchell, W. J. T. "Postcolonial Culture, Postimperial Criticism." *Transition* 56 (1992): 11–19.

Mitchell-Kernan, Claudia. "Signifying, Loud-Talking, and Marking." In *Rappin' and Stylin' Out: Communication in Urban Black America*, ed. Thomas Kochman, 315–35. Urbana: Univ. of Illinois Press, 1972.

Morrison, Toni. *The Bluest Eye*. New York: Holt, Rinehart, and Winston, 1970.

———. "Rootedness: The Ancestor as Foundation." In *Black Women Writers, 1950–1980*, ed. Mari Evans, 339–45. New York: Anchor Press, 1984.

———. *Song of Solomon*. New York: Knopf, 1977.

———. *Sula*. New York: Alfred A. Knopf, 1973.

Myers, Linda James. "The Deep Structure of Culture: Relevance of Traditional African Culture in Contemporary Life." *Journal of Black Studies* 18 (1987): 72–85.

Naylor, Gloria. *Linden Hills*. New York: Viking Penguin, 1986.

———. *Mama Day*. New York: Vintage, 1989.

———. *The Women of Brewster Place*. New York: Penguin, 1983.

Newton, Judith. "Making—and Remaking—History: Another Look at 'Patriarchy.'" In *Feminist Issues in Scholarship*, ed. Shari Benstock, 124–40. Bloomington: Indiana Univ. Press, 1987.

Niranjana, Tejaswini. *Siting Translation: History, Post-Structuralism, and the Colonial Context*. Berkeley: Univ. of California Press, 1992.

Petry, Ann. *The Street*. 1946; New York: Pyramid Books, 1976.

Pettis, Joyce. "A *MELUS* Interview: Paule Marshall." *MELUS* 17 (1992): 117–30.

Pollard, Velma. "Cultural Connections in Paule Marshall's *Praise Song* [sic] *for the Widow*." *World Literature Written in English* 25 (1985): 285–98.

Poplin, Dennis. *Communities: A Survey of Theories and Methods of Research*. New York: Macmillan, 1972.

Porter, Connie. *All-Bright Court*. New York: Harper Collins, 1991.

Pryse, Marjorie. " 'Pattern against the Sky': Deism and Motherhood in Ann Petry's *The Street*." In *Conjuring: Black Women, Fiction, and Literary Tradition*, ed. Marjorie Pryse and Hortense J. Spillers, 116–31. Bloomington: Indiana Univ. Press, 1985.

Rahming, Melvin B. *The Evolution of the West Indian's Image in the Afro-American Novel*. New York: Associated Faculty Press, 1986.

Randour, Mary Lou. *Women's Psyche, Women's Spirit*. New York: Columbia Univ. Press, 1987.

Ray, Benjamin C. *African Religions: Symbol, Ritual, and Community*. Englewood Cliffs, N.J.: Prentice Hall, 1976.

Redding, Saunders. *They Came in Chains*. Philadelphia: J. B. Lippincott, 1959.

Reimers, David. *Still the Golden Door: The Third World Comes to America*. New York: Columbia Univ. Press, 1985.

Russell, Michele. "Black-Eyed Blues Connection: Teaching Black Women II." *Women's Studies Newsletter* 5 (1977): 24–28.

Russell, Sandi. "An Interview with Paule Marshall." *Wasafiri* 8 (1988): 14–16.

Sandiford, Keith A. "Paule Marshall's *Praisesong for the Widow*: The Reluctant Heiress, or Whose Life is it Anyway?" *Black American Literature Forum* 20 (1986): 371–92.

Showalter, Elaine, ed. *The New Feminist Criticism*. New York: Pantheon, 1985.

———. "Women's Time, Women's Space: Writing the History of Feminist Criticism." In *Feminist Issues in Literary Scholarship*, ed. Shari Benstock, 30–44. Bloomington: Indiana Univ. Press, 1987.

Smith, Barbara. "Toward a Black Feminist Literary Criticism." In *The New Feminist Criticism*, ed. Elaine Showalter, 168–85. New York: Pantheon, 1985.

Smith, Michael G. *Kinship and Community in Carriacou*. New Haven, Conn.: Yale Univ. Press, 1962.

Smitherman, Geneva. *Talkin and Testifyin: The Language of Black America*. Boston: Houghton Mifflin, 1977.

Spillers, Hortense. "Chosen Place, Timeless People: Some Figurations on the New World." In *Conjuring: Black Women, Fiction, and Literary Tradition*, ed. Marjorie Pryse and Hortense Spillers, 151–75, Bloomington: Indiana Univ. Press, 1985.

———. "Cross-Currents, Discontinuities: Black Women's Fiction." In *Conjuring: Black Women, Fiction, and Literary Tradition*, ed. Marjorie Pryse and Hortense Spillers, 249–61. Bloomington: Indiana Univ. Press, 1985.

———. "A Hateful Passion, A Lost Love." In *Feminist Issues in Literary Scholarship*, ed. Shari Benstock, 181–208. Bloomington: Indiana Univ. Press, 1987.

Steiner, George. *Extraterritorial: Papers on Literature and the Language Revolution*. New York: Atheneum, 1976.

Straight, Susan. *I Been in Sorrow's Kitchen and Licked Out All the Pots*. New York: Hyperion, 1992.

Stuckey, Sterling. *Slave Culture*. New York: Oxford Univ. Press, 1987.

Talbert, L. Lee. "The Poetics of Prophecy in Paule Marshall's *Soul Clap Hands and Sing*." MELUS 5 (1978): 49–56.

Tate, Claudia. "Maya Angelou" (interview). In *Black Women Writers at Work*, 1–11. New York: Continuum, 1983.

———. "Gayl Jones" (interview). In *Black Women Writers at Work*, 89–99. New York: Continuum Press, 1983.

Taylor, Ronald L. "Psychological Modes of Adaptation." In *Black Men*, ed. Laurence Gray, 141–58. Beverly Hills, Calif.: Sage Publications, 1981.

Thelwell, Mike. "Back with the Wind: Mr. Styron and the Reverend Turner." In *William Styron's Nat Turner: Ten Black Writers Respond*, ed. John Henrik Clarke, 79–91. Boston: Beacon Press, 1968.

Toomer, Jean. *Cane*. 1923; New York: Liveright, 1975.

Turner, Darwin. Introduction to *God Bless the Child*, by Kristin Hunter, 1964; Washington, D.C.: Howard Univ. Press, 1986.

———. Introduction to *Soul Clap Hands and Sing*, by Paule Marshall. 1961; Washington, D.C.: Howard Univ. Press, 1988.

Turner, Victor. "Carnival, Ritual, and Play in Rio de Janeiro." In *Time Out of Time: Essays on the Festival*, ed. Alessandro Falassi, 74–90. Albuquerque: Univ. of New Mexico Press, 1987.

Wade-Gayles, Gloria. *No Crystal Stair: Visions of Race and Sex in Black Women's Fiction*. New York: Pilgrim Press, 1984.

Walker, Alice. *In Love and Trouble: Stories of Black Women*. New York: Harcourt Brace, 1974.

———. "Zora Neale Hurston: A Cautionary Tale and a Partisan View." In *In*

Search of Our Mothers' Gardens, 83–92. New York: Harcourt Brace Jovanovich, 1983.

Walker, Margaret. *Jubilee*. Boston: Houghton Mifflin, 1966.

Waniek, Marilyn Nelson. "Paltry Things: Immigrants and Marginal Men in Paule Marshall's Short Fiction." *Callaloo* 6 (1983): 46–56.

Washington, Mary Helen. Afterword to *Brown Girl, Brownstones*, by Paule Marshall. 1959; New York: Feminist Press, 1981.

———. " 'The Darkened Eye Restored': Notes toward a Literary History of Black Women." In *Reading Black, Reading Feminist*, ed. Henry Louis Gates, Jr., 30–43. New York: Penguin, 1990.

———. Introduction to *Black-Eyed Susans: Classic Stories by and about Black Women*, ed. Mary Helen Washington. Garden City, N.Y.: Anchor Books, 1975.

———. "New Lives and New Letters." *College English* 43 (1981): 1–1.

West, Dorothy. *The Living Is Easy*. 1948; New York: Feminist Press, 1982.

Wilentz, Gay. *Binding Cultures: Black Women Writers in Africa and the Diaspora*. Bloomington: Indiana Univ. Press, 1992.

Wilkinson, Alec. *Big Sugar: Seasons in the Cane Fields of Florida*. New York: Vintage Books, 1989.

Williams, Sherley Anne. *Dessa Rose*. New York: William Morrow, 1986.

Willis, Susan. *Specifying: Black Women Writing the American Experience*. Madison: Univ. of Wisconsin Press, 1987.

Wright, Sarah. *This Child's Gonna Live*. 1965; New York: Feminist Press, 1986.

Yeats, William B. "Vacillation." In *The Norton Anthology of Modern Poetry*, ed. Richard Ellman and Robert O'Clair, 134. New York: W. W. Norton, 1993.

Zahan, Dominique. *The Religion, Spirituality, and Thought of Traditional Africa*. Trans. Kate Ezra Martin and Lawrence M. Martin. Chicago: Univ. of Chicago Press, 1979.

Index